The Transformational Giving Playbook™

Updated Edition

The definitive guide for nonprofits that want to exponentially grow revenue and impact through six and seven-figure gifts

Lisa Scott with Pam Sterling

Book Illustrations by Stefanie Koehler

The Transformational Giving Playbook™ Updated Edition

Cover designed by Telemachus Press, LLC

Cover art and book illustrations by Stefanie Koehler

The Transformational Giving Playbook™ is a trademark of TGP Consulting LLC

Publishing Services by Telemachus Press, LLC
7652 Sawmill Road
Suite 304
Dublin, Ohio 43016
http://www.telemachuspress.com

Visit the author website:
http://www.transformationalgivingplaybook.com

Library of Congress Control Number: 2023912300

ISBN: 978-1-956867-69-5 (eBook)
ISBN: 978-1-956867-70-1 (Hardcocver)

Category: BUSINESS & ECONOMICS / Nonprofit Organizations & Charities / Fundraising & Grants

Version 2023.08.07

Praise for *The Transformational Giving Playbook*™

"As donors who pride ourselves on transformational gifts to several nonprofits, this book clearly articulates what's required to keep donors engaged and motivated to bring their like-minded friends with them. This is a must-read for any nonprofit looking to attract the donors and allies aligned with their mission."

Jonathan Lavine
Co-Managing Partner, Bain Capital, LP
and Trustee, The Crimson Lion Foundation

Jeannie Lavine
Trustee, The Crimson Lion Foundation

"Development officers, I dare you to read *The Transformational Giving Playbook*™ and not feel your heart speed up! Packed into this book is a step-by-step, comprehensive fundraising approach that empowers nonprofit organizations to become true partners with today's philanthropists. Lisa Scott is handing you the recipe for success in driving sustainable solutions-focused change."

Shannon McCracken
Chief Executive Officer, The Nonprofit Alliance

"I have seen first-hand the tremendous power of this work on a team's fundraising performance. A solid structured approach, along with thoughtful and tailored team support and clear goals, creates competence and confidence. It is deeply rewarding to lead a team in reaching further than they thought possible and succeeding in delivering the revenue needed to fund real impact. *The Transformational Giving Playbook*™ has been foundational to that."

Alyssa Herman
Chief Development Officer, The New Jewish Home

"*The Transformational Giving Playbook*™ is an innovative step-by-step masterclass that will literally transform its readers' approach to the art and science of fundraising. Grounded in real-life examples and practical systems, this book will challenge nonprofit senior leadership and development professionals alike to evaluate its philanthropic culture and to reimagine strategic donor engagement. The content in this book is required reading for the organization or individual who wants to achieve transformational fundraising success in support of the work and fulfillment of the mission."

LaShanda A. Jackson, MBA
Executive Director, Funders' Committee for Civic Participation
and Former Vice President of Development, Common Cause

"This book speaks to me like no other book I've read on fundraising! I finally found the workflows and standard operating procedures that will guide me through a stage gate process for fundraising—all music to the ears of a former corporate six sigma blackbelt turned nonprofit executive director. I am inspired to lead my program team and advisory board in partnership with my development team to new fundraising levels. Now more than ever we need these tools to raise more money to do more good in the world."

Kendra Parlock
Vice President, Partnership Development, NPower
and former Executive Director, NPower Maryland

"Lisa Scott has given a unique and valuable gift to the nonprofit sector and thereby to all of society. Her *Transformational Giving Playbook* is accessible, clear-cut, visionary, and ultimately profoundly effective. It lays out in detail the recipe for aligning the deep passions of donors with organizational missions in order to transform our world for the better."

Rosemarie Rae
Vice Chancellor-Finance and Chief Financial Officer,
UC Berkeley

"Meaningful engagement can have a transformational effect on any organization. Now more than ever, at a time when we are craving authenticity and connection, *The Transformational Giving Playbook*™ inspires us to dream big and connect with the passion and courage needed to ignite transformational change across the social good ecosystem."

Kyla Shawyer
CEO & Co-Founder, Philanthropy & Fundraising North America

"Marrying high-level theory with practical methodology, *The Transformational Giving Playbook*™ is THE definitive 'how-to' for creating the organizational culture, structure and systems that facilitate highly-coveted 6- and 7-figure giving. It answers the questions we had about transformational fundraising ... and the ones we didn't even know to ask."

Jill Vorndran
Chief Development Officer, Covenant House International

"The nonprofit sector needs a shakeup to make transformational impact at scale, and Lisa Scott has provided the detailed roadmap to do just that. If followed, *The Transformational Giving Playbook*™ will help nonprofits make exponential progress in addressing the world's most challenging issues. It holds the promise of transformation for the whole sector."

Ashley Kilpatrick
Former Chief Revenue Officer, Make-A-Wish Mid-Atlantic

"*The Transformational Giving Playbook*™ is thankfully filling two gaps that have existed for the 30 years I have worked with nonprofits. First, it provides a clear framework that goes beyond the 'donor-centered' buzzwords to balance understanding the donor, empowering the team, and holding the organizational leadership responsible for driving success. Second, it provides equally clear guidance to the nonprofit software industry who, with a couple of exceptions, have failed to understand how to harness technology for high-touch fundraising. Lisa Scott has gone from being perhaps the most effective technology consultant I know to being a pioneer in the world of truly transformational fundraising."

Peter Gross
Nonprofit Leadership Coach and Consultant

"I play many roles, but my role as a philanthropist is one of the most rewarding, as it gives me a deep sense that I can make a difference. One of the things I've learned over the years is, if you want to make an omelet you need to crack a few eggs. *The Transformational Giving Playbook*™ does an artful job of honestly and respectfully 'cracking a few eggs' by laying out the reasons nonprofits often struggle to create consistent growth and offers a powerful yet practical approach to help organizations transform from the inside out, to increase their revenue and their impact."

Chuck Longfield
Philanthropist, K-12 Education and
President, Longfield Family Foundation

"With 'Guidance, Groundwork and Gift'—*The Transformational Giving Playbook*™ hits the trifecta. This invaluable resource gives you the tools to profoundly increase your mission impact through transformational gifts. It is sure to become a classic resource for serious non-profit leaders."

Nora Frank
Former Vice President for Philanthropy, Mass Audubon

"*The Transformational Giving Playbook*™ is the perfect tool for nonprofits. Preparing for truly transformational giving takes strengthening all aspects of your organizational culture, team, and processes. This invaluable book walks you through, step-by-step, what's needed to do that. This relationship-driven approach delivers the kind of revenue that creates lasting impact."

Jill Davis
Chief Resource Development and Growth Officer, Share Our Strength

“I came to this process from a for-profit and startup background, where the sales cycle is more individualized and single-threaded—each salesperson making their own sales. What’s different about effective nonprofit fundraising is how *collaborative* it is, and how that collaboration is actually a science, not just an art. TGP made it clear how all those pieces fit together.

Alison Go
Former Chief Strategy Officer, Civic News Company

Table of Contents

Dedication

The Transformational Giving Playbook™ provides value in anytime, but we especially love this truth so beautifully and accurately captured by author and activist Arundhati Roy during this particular time in history:

> Historically, pandemics have forced humans to break with the past and imagine their world anew. This one is no different. It is a portal, a gateway between one world and the next. We can choose to walk through it, dragging the carcasses of our prejudice and hatred, our avarice, our data banks and dead ideas, our dead rivers and smoky skies behind us. Or we can walk through lightly, with little luggage, ready to imagine another world. And ready to fight for it.

Our sincere hope is that this new holistic and proven approach—firmly grounded in the power of effective processes—will enable nonprofit organizations to take the journey and transform themselves and their whole organizations by radically changing their approach to fundraising. In so doing, we also invite a life-affirming transformation of donors—by deeply connecting them to making a difference with real impact to change the world for the better.

Acknowledgements

First and foremost, to every client who's partnered with me at Barker & Scott Consulting and TGP Consulting, THANK YOU!

Thank you for choosing me to be your partner.
Thank you for being open and honest about your challenges.
Thank you for sharing all your bright spots.
My work with you laid the foundation for this book.

To The Children's Museum of Indianapolis, City Year, Civic News Company, Facing History and Ourselves, and Share Our Strength, I am grateful for your willingness to share your powerful stories with the world through this book.

Michael and Pam, thank you for articulating so well the donor side of the fundraising equation. You perfectly illustrate the 'mission magic' that happens when a donor and organization are truly aligned.

Cece, thank you for willingness to share your personal story and for demonstrating the power of story to inspire others to make a difference through their giving.

To everyone who read all or a portion of this book at some point in its iterations and whose feedback got it to where it is today, thank you. Jeremy Cramer, Lisa Eggers, Mary Beth McIntyre, Lachelle McMillan, David Scott, Charity Tubalado Jovanovic, my former Partners in Barker & Scott Consulting, Doug Barker, Alan Levine, and David Price, and most especially, Pam Sterling.

Pam, I could not have written this book without you. Your support has been greater than what I could have imagined. I learned so much from you! Thank you for always "speaking the truth in love and without judgment" (your words, which you live by) and for keeping me from playing small.

Stef Koehler, you are an amazing illustrator and, more importantly to me, you are a true friend.

—Lisa Scott

Preface to the Updated Edition

What's Changed for Me Personally

Since this book was published in 2021, I left the company I co-founded in 2002 in the good hands of my fellow Partners so I could launch a new company. My 20 years of work with Barker & Scott Consulting were immensely enjoyable, and I realized that more than the technology strategy, management, and operational work Barker & Scott is known for, the fundraising process work of *The Transformational Giving Playbook*™ is where my true passion lies. This is the work that most lights me up, so in 2022 I decided to follow my heart and begin a new endeavor.

My new company, TGP Consulting, is all about helping nonprofits exponentially grow their revenue and impact through six and seven-figure gifts.

I've seen firsthand just how powerful this work is. Transformational giving isn't just about "big money gifts." It's about transforming the impact an organization can have, while at the same time transforming the organization itself, the people within the organization, and, equally important, transforming the donors making the transformational gifts.

I'm incredibly proud of the work I did for 20 years through Barker & Scott and the strong relationships the company established with so many amazing organizations. Barker & Scott continues to excel at serving nonprofits, and in my new venture, I look forward to serving nonprofits in a different way.

What's Changed in this New Version of the Book

For starters, from a purely cosmetic perspective, the look and feel of the printed book is different. It's a smaller size and it's hard cover so it's more durable for people who are using it regularly as a reference. And the color of the cover has changed to distinguish this book from the original publication.

From a content perspective, there's new stuff!

First, we've added case studies for two additional clients, The Children's Museum of Indianapolis and Civic News Company. They are both incredibly impactful organizations that we've had the privilege of partnering with and, while they are in the early stages of their implementation of *The Transformational Giving Playbook*™, they've already realized tremendous benefits that are worth sharing with those who are reading this for the first time or in the process of your own implementation.

Second, aside from seeing minor changes throughout the book, you'll see that certain sections have been updated and new ones added. Most notably:

- Within the Guidance section, you'll find a **new comprehensive framework for Transformational Goal Setting.**
- Within the Groundwork section, in the Identification stage of the Strategic Relationship Management Cycle, **the scope of what constitutes level 1 research has been reduced**. Since level 1 research is about getting you to the Qualification stage, you only need only a minimum amount of research at this point in the cycle. Consequently, the reduced scope allows you to get to the Qualification stage much faster and decreases the time commitment on the part of your Prospect Researcher. (A big thanks to Charity Tubalado Jovanovic, founder of the prospect development firm, Heart in the Cloud, for her insights in this area).
- Within the Groundwork section, **"Conduct an exploratory conversation with the prospect"** (i.e., discovery or qualification meeting) **has been called out as an activity in the Qualification stage**, and detailed guidance has been provided for how to approach that conversation. Having this conversation early in the Strategic Relationship Management

Cycle ensures that you move into Cultivation with a prospect who warrants pursuit for a transformational gift. If you wait to do this as part of the Cultivation stage, it means you potentially will have spent a lot of time in Strategy (the stage that follows Qualification and precedes Cultivation) that could be wasted. This change enables you to know sooner rather than later if you have a qualified transformational gift prospect.

- The last change to the Groundwork section **involves significant updates to the pipeline meeting framework**. Because pipeline meetings are such an important tool for your organization, a fuller description has been provided for who should attend and the role they should play, how to prepare, how to approach facilitation, and what guiding principles you want to consider to ensure the best participation and outcomes.

- Finally, just about every **blueprint, template, and guide has been revised**, and there is space for you to record critical details about your prospects, like the name, CRM record ID number, etc. Additionally, you'll find a new Curated Connection Experience Planning Template and Solicitation Meeting Planning Template to accompany those respective blueprints. Lastly, you'll find a bonus Board Member Questionnaire to help you understand a board member's network so you can determine how to approach prospecting with that board member and to help you assess their comfort with fundraising so you can determine how to best leverage them in your fundraising efforts. You can access these new templates and all the others at:

transformationalgivingplaybook.com/TGPtemplates

Foreword

A good friend and colleague often reminds me . . .

There are many more important things than money, but they all cost money.

I've been fortunate for the past 25 years to have a career that's been focused on the "many more important things."

Finding a cure for ALS; strengthening families and communities by fighting for livable wages, good schools, and healthy environments; helping kids stay in school and fighting the national dropout crisis; using lessons of history to challenge teachers and their students to stand up to bigotry and hate.

It's been incredibly rewarding work.

Equally rewarding though, has been the privilege of being surrounded by and learning from extraordinary philanthropists—business and community leaders who trusted me to ensure that their hard-earned money made the difference they wanted to make at The ALS Therapy Development Institute, The United Way, City Year, and Facing History and Ourselves. I realized, in the process, that the nonprofit became the conduit for those philanthropists to become their best selves, and who they were called to be.

The lessons I've learned from this work and from these philanthropic relationships have changed me. They've shaped my leadership doctrine, my management philosophy, and I am undoubtedly a better partner to my wife and father to my children because of it.

That's why I was so excited to hear that Lisa was writing this book, because I've experienced firsthand how transformational giving is *transformational* on so many levels. It transforms the impact the organization can have; it transforms the organization itself, the philanthropist, and yes, even the fundraiser.

I first met Lisa Scott and Doug Barker (Founders of Barker & Scott Consulting) when we were implementing a new donor management system at City Year ahead of our 25th anniversary campaign. I had recently joined City Year as their Vice President of Major Gifts.

Like many nonprofits, City Year's major gift fundraising relied heavily on the "art" of fundraising—individual superstars who had a natural talent for fundraising. Where we needed help was on better defining and implementing the "science" of fundraising—clearly defined strategies and business processes so that we could configure the donor management system accordingly and everyone could contribute to the fundraising success of the organization.

We thought that's what we were hiring Barker & Scott to help us implement—which they did. But what they delivered was so much more than we ever expected, and the result they helped us create was beyond our wildest dreams.

The Process

Lisa and Doug brought us on an organizational journey.

They brought everyone together to create a collective understanding of where the organization was and what we could become.

They were incredibly sensitive to culture and organizational dynamics and were able to engage everyone's passion for making an impact on the mission and use it as a driver for organizational change.

They had respect for the art of fundraising, while helping us recognize the power of science to elevate the art, and they created a safe space for everyone to grow together to use the best of both.

Through their expert facilitation and high emotional intelligence, they helped us recognize that the opportunity for us was about much more than a new set of business processes. Rather, it was about individual and organizational change, which meant meaningful engagement of all the key players: the board, executive team, senior leadership throughout the organization, as well as Development. All went on a journey to discover their best selves and how they can continue to truly transform themselves to have much greater impact as an organization.

The Product

What Barker & Scott helped us create out of that process was the very first *Major Gifts Playbook* (precursor to *The Transformational Giving Playbook*™). The reputation of Barker & Scott's commitment to excellence preceded them, but what they delivered blew us away. The precision and yet practicality of *The Playbook* was exceptional and it became an invaluable guide for creating extraordinary results (more on that later).

In addition, *The Playbook* delivered some unexpected things.

It created a greater level of **confidence** for our team members, because they had clear guidelines for their role on the team and a common understanding of the measures of success.

It helped create a greater sense of **community** among our staff. Colleagues who had not been involved in fundraising in the past, but who could be a major asset, were brought into the fold and were recognized and rewarded for the value they brought.

Finally, it helped **change mental models**. At City Year, in conjunction with *The Playbook*, we launched a new giving community called the Red Jacket Society. The entry level for the Society was $10,000, and we had several higher dollar levels above that. At first, many staff were concerned that their donors didn't have that capacity. We invited them to think bigger. The truth—and what we ultimately demonstrated—is there is high-value philanthropy everywhere, but you need a good process, the skills, the confidence in the mission, and a bold vision to make a bold Ask.

The Payoff

If we stopped right here, the benefit to the organization would have been immense. But, of course, we're fundraisers, and raising more money so our organization could further scale its impact is what we're all about.

So, what was the result?

The Playbook and the development of the Red Jacket Society program enabled City Year to significantly expand its Major Gifts program in support of an ambitious organizational plan to serve more students across the country. This contributed to our ability to increase operating revenue at City Year from $114 million to $153 million within four years—a 34% increase. On top of that, we exceeded our 25th anniversary campaign goal of $150 million and brought in $157 million.

All of this dramatically increased our ability to serve in more cities to create improved outcomes for students in systemically under-resourced schools, and to cultivate the next generation of leaders through our alumni. In other words, we got to make a difference in more kids' lives, which ultimately benefits all of us.

Given our results at City Year, when I then went to Facing History and Ourselves, there was no question I had to bring Barker & Scott with me. Once again, the implementation of *The Playbook* at Facing History created extraordinary results. Our revenue went from $19 million to $24 million in 12 months, and with the help of several multi-year commitments that were already underway, we hit an organizational high of $31 million in 18 months. The growth in revenue enabled us to grow the number of educators served from 2,000 to over 30,000 per year. This dramatically increased our ability to inspire students all over the world to become upstanders and stand up to bigotry and hate.

All of this is to say that I believe *The Transformational Giving Playbook*™ brings a powerful new perspective, focus, and approach to nonprofit fundraising.

Not only is it a literal "how to" guide for transformational gift fundraising; it also empowers fundraisers to be their authentic selves and to bring their passion and creativity to everything they do, while being grounded in the science of strategic relationship management.

The Transformational Giving Playbook™ provides a methodology that creates an exceptional philanthropic experience for the donor and enables your nonprofit to attract the brightest and best philanthropists.

It's the multimillion-dollar idea every nonprofit should adopt.

Jeremy Cramer
CEO, Exponential Philanthropy

The Transformational Giving Playbook™
Updated Edition

Introduction

We wrote this book for one reason and one reason only—to help nonprofits raise more money to do more good.

This book is all about you, and helping your organization get the resources it needs to accomplish its mission.

Imagine …

> Ensuring everyone has access to clean water.
>
> Lifting 1 million children out of poverty in your lifetime.
>
> Saving the Asian elephant from extinction.
>
> Putting an end to domestic violence.
>
> Ending mass incarceration of people of color in the U.S.
>
> Finding a cure for Alzheimer's disease.
>
> Securing full equality and protections for trans people and all LGBTQ communities.

These things and more are possible. And if you want this too, you have the book in your hands that will show you how to get there.

The Bold Vision

The Transformational Giving Playbook™ shows you, with real-life examples, how to go **from incremental, stagnant, or negative growth**—where your organization is struggling to raise money for your mission, putting your organization, your staff, and the mission at risk—**to exponential growth**, where you are raising significantly more money through a focus on six and seven-figure transformational gifts, which ultimately provides the capacity to do WAY more good.

In this book we offer a completely new comprehensive approach to major gift, corporate, and foundation fundraising that not only transforms nonprofit organizations but transforms the people within the organization and the givers themselves.

The Problem

But in order to understand the solution, we must first understand the problem.

The nonprofit sector is critical to the well-being of all life on the planet, yet raising money within nonprofits has become increasingly more difficult. Many are struggling to create incremental growth at best, save for a momentary crisis that serves as a temporary rallying cry. Consequently, nonprofits all too often can't make the impact they need to make at the level and at the speed they need to make it.

So why is it that so many large, and even prestigious, organizations are struggling to raise enough money? We believe there are ten main contributing factors:

1. **A heavy reliance on the art of fundraising vs. the science**

   When it comes to securing transformational gifts, fundraisers often cite the ability to be creative and personable as the keys to success. Many fundraisers rely on artful elements like intuition, charm, a sense of timing, and an understanding of their geographic region's unique culture to land big gifts. They have little time and patience for the rigor that research, strategy development, and coordination with other staff, departments, and offices requires—despite knowing these scientific methods work.

2. **A belief that strong case materials (extrinsic motivators) can solve all fundraising problems**

Many fundraisers are convinced that if they only had the right case materials to convey the importance of the mission—what the organization has accomplished and what the organization needs to meet its goals—they could win over more donors. And if someone would just take that on and deliver content and templates that fundraisers can tweak, they would raise more money.

While case materials are important and helpful, extrinsic motivation alone is far from sufficient to compel donors to give at their capacity.

3. **Too much dependence on fundraising "superstars"**

At every nonprofit there are fundraisers who are presented as a model for others to follow. Often, they are assigned the top prospects and donors and are relied on to raise the bulk of the revenue for the department. but when they leave, it creates major problems for the organization. Revenue takes a hit, and it can take months to recover—especially if the superstar was an artful fundraiser who didn't document all they knew about their donors or leave a complete record of their work for the next fundraiser to build off.

4. **Lack of training and models for new, inexperienced fundraisers**

As budgets tighten, nonprofits are relying more and more on inexperienced staff to fundraise because the salaries they offer don't attract seasoned fundraisers. So, either staff with minimal experience get hired, or nonprofits take program staff who are enthusiastic and have great passion for the mission and convert them into fundraisers.

But when there is no training and no models in place to guide them, inexperienced fundraisers are left to figure things out on their own. As a result, they often flounder, reinvent the wheel, struggle to make the best sense of guidance obtained from peers, and end up being less effective than they should be.

5. **Too much time spent going after gifts that are too small to be transformational**

Many fundraisers spend too much time going after gifts that are too small to be transformational to the organization and/or they apply the same treatment to every donor regardless of the size of their giving capacity.

An inability to carefully prioritize how they spend their time and tailor the donor experience means fundraisers won't generate the transformational gifts required to move the needle on the mission in a significant way. Ten $10K-$25K gifts, while great, does not have the same impact as one $1 million gift.

6. **Business processes that don't work**

Fundraisers are often unable to articulate their organization's business processes for high-touch fundraising. Many will say "we do Moves Management," but there's a good chance they can't tell you exactly what they're expected to do in each stage of the cycle. They might not even agree on the cycle. Moreover, there's a high probability that whatever processes are in place aren't optimized for the operational needs and mission outcomes of the organization.

Without clearly defined business processes, you end up in a situation where no one does things the same way, no one knows the best way, people aren't always sure what they should be doing, and no one understands how their actions impact others. Moreover, information doesn't flow where it needs to, people are not speaking the same fundraising language, and decisions get made that aren't aligned to the overall strategy of the organization. All this puts the organization and donor relationship at risk.

7. **Lack of the right tools to effectively perform their jobs**

Fundraisers have been shooting from the hip when it comes to prioritizing their fundraising efforts and assessing their progress. In organizations where the CRM system is not fully aligned to fundraisers' needs, it becomes too much of a burden, so the bare minimum gets recorded and Excel spreadsheets and Word documents become the primary "tools" individual fundraisers and teams rely on. But Excel and Word are insufficient to analyze progress and direct the day-to-day efforts of individual fundraisers, which makes fundraising less effective for the organization as a whole.

8. A deeply ingrained "my donor" mindset

Within nonprofits it's often "every man (department, chapter, affiliate, site, regional office, state office, headquarters) for himself." Many fundraisers keep "their" donors close to the vest and are unwilling to share data and information with other departments or locations, even when there's an understanding or a sense the donor might have a broader connection to the organization.

Intuitively we know this is problematic. It would be like every individual branch of a bank only knowing what a person or organization does at that branch, and not being able to understand the fullness and scope of the customer banking relationship to serve them accordingly. Yet, fundraisers actively work, and are too often encouraged by management, to "wall off" their donors, creating winners and losers.

We know why this happens: organizational and budget structures require that each department and location raise funds to cover their operating expenses, so an 'I have to protect my territory' or an 'I have to do what it takes to make my numbers' attitude is the natural, and unfortunate, consequence.

9. Reluctance of program staff to support fundraising efforts

Fundraising staff are responsible for raising money, but they rely on program staff to share in that responsibility by writing content for grant applications and impact reports, giving donors a meaningful programmatic experience, and sometimes implementing a donor's grand idea or pet project, which may deviate from the organization's programmatic priorities. But program staff receive little to no recognition for the work they do to support fundraising, which creates tension. This tension builds over time and makes program staff less inclined to be willing partners, but the truth is, the entire team is in this together because programs can't exist without revenue to fuel them.

10. **Board members engaged to fundraise who don't pull their full weight**

    Nonprofits often recruit of board members with domain expertise or name recognition as well as high-net-worth individuals who can give or get transformational gifts. But sometimes, those who are engaged to support fundraising efforts don't pull their full weight.

    When this happens, the board doesn't move the organization far enough along in delivering on its mission—which is the very thing boards are supposed to do—so fundraisers and senior leaders end up spending an extraordinary amount of their limited time keeping board members happy and engaged without the financial payoff to the organization that makes it worthwhile.

All of these problems make it increasingly difficult to raise the kinds of funds that are necessary to solve the problems you're here to solve and make the kind of difference you are here to make. The impact is often felt among fundraisers themselves—feeling stressed, frustrated, fearful and heartbroken. What draws us to nonprofits are the missions, and when we can't make the difference we want to make, as quickly as we want to do it, it is hard on everyone.

The Stats

If any of this sounds like the story of your organization, if any of these problems sound familiar, we want you to know that you are not alone. Across the nonprofit sector, organizations have been experiencing incremental growth, at best, for years. And this is largely because **growth in charitable giving on the whole has been incremental**.

This points to the need for a different approach—one that can help an organization break free from this trend in order to achieve its mission.

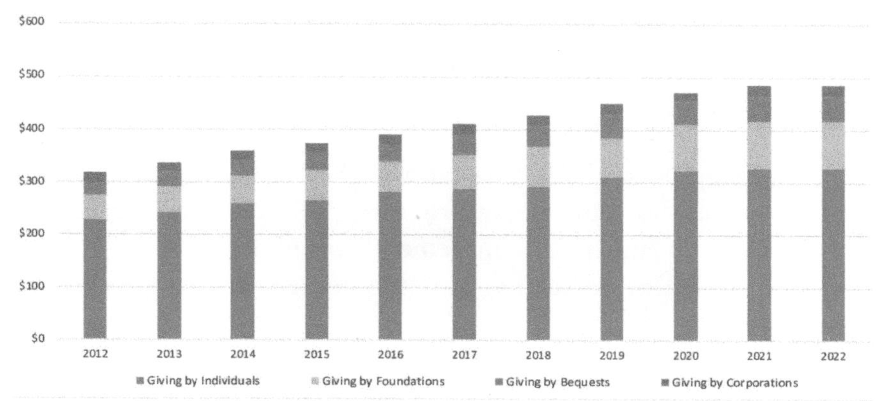

Source of data: Giving USA Foundation

Why It Matters

Why does it matter that you chart a new path away from incremental growth to exponential growth?

Nonprofits are uniquely positioned to do the work no commercial enterprises or governmental bodies can do. Nonprofits are the organizations most willing, committed, and intentional about solving the world's greatest and most intractable problems.

Without nonprofits we cannot end hunger and food insecurity. Without nonprofits we cannot find the cures to devastating diseases like Alzheimer's, cancer, and multiple sclerosis. Without nonprofits we cannot undo the damaging effects of systemic racism. Without nonprofits we cannot equip every child with the education they need to succeed in the world. Without nonprofits we cannot end the physical and emotional abuse of people and animals. Without nonprofits we cannot stop climate change.

These are some of the most defining issues of our time and solving them can't take 30, 20 or even 10 years. We need solutions now and nonprofits are best equipped to deliver them.

So, it matters that nonprofits move from incremental growth to exponential growth. The health of our communities, our nations, and the whole of the planet depends on you succeeding in your mission.

Our Story

In 2002, Doug Barker left his position as CIO and Lisa Scott (author) left her position as Director of Systems Applications at The Nature Conservancy to launch a management consulting and technology strategy firm, Barker & Scott Consulting, to help more nonprofits do more good.

At Barker & Scott, we had the privilege of working closely with nearly 100 nonprofits to increase their fundraising and mission success. These organizations ranged in annual revenues from over $1 billion to under $1 million, and their missions encompassed everything from arts, culture and humanities, education and research, environmental and animal welfare, health, human services, international development and relief, to public and societal benefit sectors.

Our experience gave us an in-depth understanding of the strategic and operational needs ACROSS ALL fundraising business units—from Direct Marketing to Major and Planned Gifts, to Corporate Partnerships and Foundation Relations, to Gift Processing—and a unique understanding of all aspects of fundraising and constituent relationship management strategies and systems. And we learned what works to make fundraisers more effective and create a culture of philanthropy that extends throughout the organization and leads to transformational growth.

Our experience with some of the world's finest, largest, and most prestigious nonprofits also gave us in-depth insights into how nonprofits really work.

We've seen the beautiful, the bad, and the ugly from the inside out.

After 20 years in the nonprofit space, we started to notice a disturbing trend among many of our clients …

Raising money within nonprofits was becoming increasingly more difficult, putting missions, staff, and organizations at risk.

We recognized that nonprofits were competing with more and more organizations *with* similar missions, and that organizational and budget structures often created a situation where fundraising departments and chapters within the same organization ended up competing against one another, creating winners and losers.

This external and internal competition created a disjointed experience for donors that encumbered securing gifts at capacity. Hence, fundraising growth became incremental at best.

In 2013, we had an experience that changed everything.

City Year is an education nonprofit organization in Boston, dedicated to helping students and schools succeed.

Prior to 2013, City Year had focused its fundraising efforts primarily on corporations, some foundations, and also received some money from school districts and the federal AmeriCorps program. While the organization had strong support from individuals supporting City Year locations across the country, it did not have a unified Major Gifts program.

In 2013, City Year set out to change that.

Under the leadership of the CEO and Chief Alumni & Advancement Officer, and as part of the five-year 25th anniversary fundraising campaign, City Year set a goal to grow the number and size of major gifts. To achieve that, they brought in a new VP of Major Gifts, migrated to a new, more robust CRM, and assembled a Prospect Research team for the first time ever. Everyone at the National Office was on board and excited to implement a new Major Gifts program.

That's when they called Barker & Scott.

With the implementation of the new CRM, City Year needed help defining their business processes, so they could configure the new database to support those processes.

Barker & Scott worked closely with the City Year staff at both the national and local levels from across the country to define clear business processes and produce a set of tools that included a comprehensive prospect and donor pipeline system with regular Pipeline Meetings, guidelines for Cultivation Teams, new performance measures, and guiding principles for how the team interacts with each other and their donors. All of this was documented in what we called the "Major Gifts Playbook."

> *"This was the first time we put the art AND the science of fundraising together."*
>
> ~ Charity Tubalado Jovanovic,
> Senior Prospect Development Director

The Result

City Year exceeded their expectations … BY A LOT!

Within just four years, City Year made significant strides in its Major Gift fundraising efforts.

The extraordinary growth in Major Gifts revenue came primarily from two sources:

1. The launching of the Red Jacket Society, which enabled City Year to more than double the number of $10K+ donors, and the creation of a $100K Platinum giving level within the Red Jacket Society, which allowed City Year to go from very few to fifty $100K+ donors. The remarkable thing about this is that most of these donors came from their already established donor pool.

2. An increase in the number of transformational gifts—from a handful of gifts of $1 million or more in 2013, mostly from corporate partners and some foundations—to over two dozen gifts of $1 million or more. These new, extraordinary gifts come from not just corporations and foundations, but individuals too.

Charity Tubulado Jovanovic, Senior Prospect Development Director, sums it up this way …

> *"The Playbook helped develop the "muscle" for $1M+ gifts … Most of the $100K donors were already in our donor pool, but the staff just didn't have the mindset, the skills, the confidence, or the tools to get to higher levels of giving. The Playbook was a powerful tool that helped us maximize our Major Gifts potential."*

But City Year didn't just stop at transforming Major Gifts. Through an internal focus on impact and adoption of best-in-class fundraising practices across the board, City Year grew funding from its other sources—federal AmeriCorps program, local school districts, and other private contributions from corporations and foundations. By transforming fundraising on the whole, City Year was able to increase its operating revenue from $114 million to $153 million. On top of that, they exceeded their 25th anniversary campaign goal of $150 million and brought in $157 million.

With this foundation, City Year has been able to encourage deeper investments into the community from its donors, and to make visible the triad of supporters that make the organization's work possible: AmeriCorps, district and local funding, and private donors.

But could this same result be recreated at other organizations? Or was it just a fluke?

That's when the VP of Major Gifts at City Year went to Facing History and Ourselves (Facing History) to serve as their Chief Development Officer. Facing History is an education nonprofit that uses lessons of history to challenge teachers and their students to stand up to bigotry and hate.

Facing History was undergoing a major transition from a founder-led organization to a new CEO, a new board of directors, and a new strategic plan. At the time, Facing History had about 50,000 educators that had been trained and they were adding about 2,000 per year. With their new CEO, new board and new strategic plan, they set out to achieve an ambitious, seemingly impossible goal of adding 150,000 new educators (for a total of 200,000) over the next five years. This meant increasing from an additional 2,000 educators per year, to adding 30,000 per year.

Given the success of The Playbook at City Year, Jeremy Cramer knew he wanted to also elevate the art of fundraising at Facing History with the science and precision that had been implemented at City Year, so he called us in 2016.

We created a Playbook unique to Facing History that laid out a detailed plan for relationship management, Cultivation Teams, Cultivation Strategies, Pipeline Meetings, staff training, common goals and guiding principles, as well as clear performance measures.

In addition to the Playbook, Facing History had three key factors in place.

First, they had an inspirational leader in their CEO—Roger Brooks. Roger is kind, approachable, seeks input and listens, and then trusts his team to execute; he doesn't micromanage. Roger is a role model and an excellent fundraiser. As a result, he is deeply respected by both the staff and the board at Facing History.

Second, they had a comprehensive strategic plan. This was an organization-wide initiative and there was clear understanding that everyone needed to be on board—from the leadership, to the staff, to the board members—and they were.

Third, they had an inspirational goal—to go from 50,000 educators to 200,000. Big goals inspire people to think and act bigger, bolder and better—which led to an unprecedented result.

The Result

What happened was extraordinary.

When staff and board members realized the impact they could have with 200,000 educators, it generated a lot of energy and excitement, and it inspired everyone to be bolder and take more risks. Most importantly though, when donors realized the impact their dollars could have on advancing the work of social justice if they achieved that goal, it inspired them give more. Many donors doubled their gifts and some multiplied their giving as much as 10 times. Remarkably, donors—individuals, foundations, and corporations alike—began to challenge EACH OTHER to give more and match each other's donations.

As a result, Facing History, like City Year, exceeded their expectations.

Their revenue grew from $19 million to $24 million in 12 months. And, with the help of several multi-year commitments that were already underway, they hit an organizational high of $31 million in 18 months. 60% of their revenue came from "transformational" gifts of at least $100K. In addition, Facing History exceeded their goal of 200,000 educators by the end of their five-year campaign, and as of this publication has partnered with over 400,000 educators around the world.

The cherry on top is that this turnaround led Facing History to have the highest number of net assets (annual fund plus endowment)—$52 million—in the organization's 42-year history.

Aha! Moment

That's when we realized we were on to something. We realized this wasn't a fluke at all, but rather, we had stumbled upon a completely new comprehensive approach to fundraising—one that had the potential to exponentially transform the impact of an organization. And this was something we needed to share with as many nonprofits as we could.

The System

So I (Lisa) partnered with Pam Sterling to codify what we learned and create *The Transformational Giving Playbook*™.

This new comprehensive approach to fundraising is one that …

- Brings the entire organization together around a common set of values, goals and leadership principles.

- Pairs the best of what we know about the art of fundraising with the best of what we know about the science of fundraising.
- Builds both the organizational and personal infrastructure required for fundraising success.
- Puts the donor's motivations and aspirations front and center.
- Equips everyone in the organization to be a winner.

If you've struggled to **raise more money to support your mission, the ONLY reason** is that one or more of the key components of *The Transformational Giving Playbook*™ are either missing or incomplete. Get these components in place in your organization, and it will transform your fundraising.

Having *The Transformational Giving Playbook*™ in place is the key to equipping your organization with the business processes, skills, and tools you need to:

- **Confidently cultivate and close** transformational gifts.
- **Align donor motivations and aspirations** with the organization's impact, transforming both in the process.
- **Prioritize your fundraising efforts** to realize more transformational gifts.
- **Create a culture of philanthropy** where every department is working together to achieve the greatest philanthropic outcome for the organization and create the greatest philanthropic experience for the donor.
- **Collaborate between national and local office**s to enthusiastically raise money and grow the prospect pipeline together.
- **Cultivate donors who continue to give at capacity** because your organization has provided a deeply satisfying philanthropic experience that enables them to make a

difference they can only make through the unique apparatus of your organization.

This means:

- No more feeling like you are on your own to figure out how to "close" a big donor.
- No more fear of making the Ask because you don't know if it's the right funding opportunity, the right amount, the right time.
- No more being overwhelmed by the sheer number of prospects in your organization's portfolio and fundraisers not knowing where to focus their energy.
- No more struggling to engage programmatic and administrative staff in fundraising efforts.
- No more competing for dollars within your own organization.
- No more working your tails off to eke out a nominal increase in giving over last year.

None of that. Just a completely new approach that enables you to transform your organization, your teams, your donors, and most importantly, your ability to make the difference you are here to make by focusing on implementing a comprehensive transformational giving program.

With that said, we'll spend the rest of the book, focused on unpacking *The Transformational Giving Playbook*™ in order to give you actionable steps you can take right away, to begin transforming your Major Gifts, Corporate, and Foundation fundraising.

The Transformational Giving Playbook™

Who is *The Transformational Giving Playbook*™ For?

As a starting point, it's important to understand that *The Transformational Giving Playbook*™ is not designed for every nonprofit. While smaller nonprofit organizations can find value in the fundamentals of the approach, *The Transformational Giving Playbook*™ is specifically designed for U.S. based nonprofits that:

1. Have annual revenues of **$10 million and up**,
2. Are **seeking transformational gifts** in the six and seven-figure range **from high-net-worth individuals (inclusive of couples and families), corporations, and foundations**[1], and
3. Have a **prospect research function**, whether in-house or outsourced.

It works particularly well for nonprofits that are **federated** (e.g., a national or international nonprofit with a headquarters in one location and multiple chapters, affiliates, sites, state offices, regional offices, etc. in other locations).

What this means is that *The Transformational Giving Playbook*™ is not designed for smaller nonprofits, or nonprofits run by volunteers, with only one or two fundraisers. Having said this, the principles, processes, and methods herein can provide value to all nonprofit organizations regardless of size.

Overview

There are three key components of *The Transformational Giving Playbook*™: Guidance, Groundwork, and Gift. Each component transforms a different aspect of the nonprofit. And all work together to transform the impact of the organization—the organization's ability to do more good and make a bigger difference.

We'll do a brief overview of each component here, then take a deeper dive into each in the following chapters.

Guidance

The first component is Guidance. Guidance transforms the Organization. The Guidance component is a recognition from the leadership of the organization that a focus on transformational giving and building out a transformational giving approach to high-touch fundraising is not just something that Development "owns" and does, but rather, it is something that must be owned by the entire organization ... because it impacts the entire organization and its mission. When an organization sets out to implement *The Transformational Giving Playbook*™, they indeed set out on a journey that will transform the organization as a whole.

There are three key elements within Guidance:

Transformational Leadership

Transformational Leaders are those who are able to effectively guide and inspire others through change. Transformational Leaders—executives as well as board members—understand that and are prepared to do whatever is required to lead their organizations, both as a guide and as a role model, through the type of change required to embrace this transformational approach to high-touch fundraising.

Transformational Goal Setting

Transformational Goal Setting provides targets that inspire organizations to rally around not just one specific target, but rather a range of good/better/best targets that inspire teams to "go the extra mile" and "do the impossible" to hit even higher goals. Transformational Goal Setting not only motivates teams to achieve the "even better still", it also encourages organizational leaders to think bigger, and inspires donors to give more to have a bigger impact.

Transformational Principles

Having a shared set of Guiding Principles for Fundraising is a key part of the organization's staff moving forward together as one, to raise more money and do more good. This is why working with the leadership and team members to establish Guiding Principles for Fundraising—that align to the organization's core values—at the beginning of a Transformational Giving Playbook project is essential to its success.

Groundwork

Next comes the Groundwork. This is all about the nitty-gritty. Groundwork transforms the Team. Make no mistake about it, the organization changes only as much as the people within it change. The elements we focus on in this part of *The Transformational Giving Playbook*™ are what equips everyone to be a winner.

Transformational System

The Strategic Relationship Management System in many ways is the "meat and potatoes" of *The Transformational Giving Playbook*™. This is where we define clear stages that each donor moves through on the way to a transformational gift: who is responsible for each stage of the relationship, what actions should be taking place at each stage, and who executes those actions. The Transformational System is what elevates the art of fundraising by applying the science of relationship management in a clear, strategic, step-by-step, and empowering way. The System also very much recognizes the power of teamwork. Much more on this to come.

Transformational Skill Set

The Transformational Skill Set component of *The Transformational Giving Playbook*™ is based on the belief that success as a high-touch fundraiser does not require superstar talent that some have and some don't. Rather it requires a high-touch fundraising skill set that can be taught and learned. Team members can be equipped with these skills through conversation scripts, role-playing, and training on everything from managing donors through the Strategic Relationship Management Cycle to leading a Transformational Gifts Pipeline Meeting. One of the most exciting methods for teaching this transformational skill set leverages the fundraising superstars in your organization as mentors to the newer members of the team. In this way, everyone is empowered to be a winner.

Transformational Tools

The right tools in the right hands are what enable us to better perform the tasks of our trade. The same is true for high-touch fundraisers. Report designs, templates, frameworks, meeting agendas, protocols, and a well-configured CRM are all examples of Transformational Tools that empower team members to succeed.

Gift

Of course, it is the transformational gift that ultimately transforms your impact as an organization. But it is often overlooked how much the gift transforms the Giver—especially when fundraisers understand and align to what matters most to the donor. For a donor to give at capacity, their gift needs to be aligned in three important ways:

Aligned to The Giver's Motivations

Understanding the giver's motivations and helping them see how their gift can help them fulfill this purpose, is the first way that the donor needs to feel aligned. For individuals, motivations are very much centered on what gives their life purpose and meaning. For corporations, motivations are often rooted in the company's corporate social responsibility business objectives. For foundations, it can be either or both.

Aligned to the Giver's Aspirations

Understanding the giver's aspirations—that is, who they aspire to be or how they aspire to be seen, what they aspire to do, and the legacy they seek to leave, and helping them see how their gift can fulfill those aspirations—is the second way that the donor needs to feel aligned.

Aligned to the Organization's Mission

The third way in which the donor needs to feel aligned is in understanding how the mission of the organization aligns with their motivations and aspirations. It is imperative that nonprofits demonstrate how the mission and the mission delivery apparatus of the organization can help the donor fulfill both their motivations and aspirations in a way they never could on their own. It is in this way that the organization gives the donor an opportunity to be the person (or organization) they've always wanted to be, and a champion to a cause they believe in.

Why The Playbook Works

So, why is it that *The Transformational Giving Playbook*™ works to help you raise more money and do more good? Why does it have the potential to transform your high-touch fundraising from incremental gains year over year, to exponential growth?

Here are the reasons why *The Transformational Giving Playbook*™ works:

1. **It elevates the art of fundraising by leveraging science** and proven strategies, as well as innovative technology, research, tools, and clearly defined business processes.

2. **It focuses on understanding and aligning to the intrinsic motivations and aspirations of the donor** and demonstrating how the mission and apparatus of the organization can help the donor fulfill both, in a way they never could on their own.

3. **It positions "superstars" to become invaluable guides by becoming mentors** to their peers, sharing their best practices, and leading knowledge-sharing sessions.

4. **It equips fundraising staff with the skill set they need** to be a successful member of the Transformational Giving team—through training, mentorship, step-by-step roadmaps and skill building.

5. **It prioritizes the time, energy and efforts of the Development department** on donors who have the capacity to give truly

transformational gifts.

6. **It provides clear business processes**, standards, expectations, accountability, and coordination designed for everyone to win.
7. **It provides fundraisers with a comprehensive set of leading-edge tools** that provide consistency, transparency, and effectiveness in fundraising efforts across the organization.
8. **It creates a unified donor experience** that significantly grows revenue across the whole of the organization and where team members work collaboratively toward a common goal—to raise more money and do more good.
9. **It creates a culture of philanthropy** where every staff person understands, appreciates, and is recognized and rewarded for how they contribute to the financial health of the organization.
10. **It prioritizes buy-in and leadership from the organization** executives and board members as a prerequisite to the success of the transformational giving program.

It is a clear, powerful, empowering, organization-wide approach that transforms the organization, transforms the teams, transforms the donors, and most importantly, transforms your ability to fulfill your mission.

What Makes This Approach Different

In order for an organization to transform its fundraising, there needs to be two shifts—a shift in the organization, and a shift in its people. Both need to grow, transform, and change for a Transformational Giving Program to succeed.

That's why **woven throughout the framework of the Playbook, there are two threads**—one focused on transforming the **Institutional Infrastructure** and the other focused on transforming the **Individual Infrastructure**.

The Institutional Infrastructure begins with a bold vision of what's possible for the organization and is built through a state-of-the-art system for transformational gift fundraising that is undergirded by a set of powerful tools to support fundraisers in closing six and seven-figure gifts. Although some solutions may stop there, we realize that transforming the Institutional Infrastructure alone is not enough to have a successful Transformational Giving Program.

If we stopped there, it would be like giving you a high-performance, state-of-the-art race car, without equipping your team with what they need to be championship race car drivers.

That's why the second thread woven throughout the framework is so important—the Individual Infrastructure. Only with the inclusion of coaching, mentorship, and skills training, will your team be empowered to believe, think, and act like "championship race car drivers."

That's what makes *The Transformational Giving Playbook*™ approach different and why it is so powerful for transforming an organization's ability to create exponential growth through transformational gifts—**we give you a state-of-the-art system for transformational gift fundraising and train your team to believe, think, and act like superstar fundraisers**.

Case Study: Civic News Company

Amy Rosenblum,
Chief Revenue Officer & CJ Ortuño, VP of Philanthropy

"Fundraising is a team sport, and you gave us the playbook."
~ Amy Rosenblum

"The Playbook was such a gift and a launchpad for me as a new leader coming in. I think it saved us at least a year of work we would have had to do on our own."
~ Amy Rosenblum

There are so many ways we benefited from this good work, including:

- Having a common language to ground us in a shared reality.
- Learning to ask a different set of questions that enable us to be more intentional.
- Shifting our pipeline meetings to a framework that encourages *strategic* discussion.
- Creating a culture of philanthropy throughout the entire organization.
- Giving us a roadmap for supporting the team through major change.

Common Language

Having a common language has been really important. First, just having a shared definition of terms has brought us together. Second, having a clear differentiation of stages within the Strategic Relationship Management Cycle has been important to helping us manage donor relationships. We're now grounded in clear expectations around what it means to be in each stage and the probability associated with that stage. We're a long way from the "possible/likely" approach we used to use.

A Different Set of Questions

With the focus on the prospect's passions, motivations, and aspirations, we've learned to ask a different set of questions. Instead of asking "How much money do we need to close the gap?" Now we're asking, "What are they interested in? What are their passions? What kind of impact do they want their philanthropy to have and how can we help them do that through our work at Civic News Company?". This enables everyone to be much more intentional and thoughtful about their cultivation efforts. We now have the same north star: "What is the most potent next step we can take to move the relationship toward a philanthropic outcome?".

Pipeline Meetings

Our pipeline meetings used to be a list of upcoming proposals and we'd go one by one, focused on due dates and timing, but not so much on strategy. Now our meetings are much more strategically driven and centered on donor relationships. Development Directors are expected to come with their top prospects and share their thinking about the approach for those opportunities and bring their strategic questions. We spend a couple hours each week on next actions based on the motivations and aspirations of the donor. In all honesty, this kind of change felt uncomfortable for some at first, as it required learning a new skill set and building a new muscle, but it has paid off as our fundraising results have begun to shift.

Culture of Philanthropy

Historically, program staff had not been involved in fundraising. But since implementing the TGP Cultivation Team structure that includes the role of Program Partner, engagement with the program staff has been great. Our program staff know their work the best, and we've opened the doors to let them share that brilliance. Now they join us in our cultivation strategy meetings and share the impacts they've had and their priorities so that everyone is on the same page. They value their roles on those teams and have embraced the whole idea of a "culture of philanthropy" so much that they are going to donor meetings with us. The same is true for our leadership team, including our Chief Strategy Officer, Chief People Officer, Chief Financial Officer, and Editor-in-Chief, and our board members, who have filled the role of Natural Partners. Our 'team sport' approach to fundraising has enabled everyone to shine in their areas of expertise.

Roadmap for Change Management

A bonus of our TGP project is that it provided a roadmap to help us with change management. We wanted to move the team to a future they couldn't yet see themselves in, and the TGP gave us a picture of what our future fundraising looks like and the opportunity for everyone to self-assess and figure out where they can grow to close the gap between where they are now and where they need to be. We're making that future vision a reality.

~~~~

Knowing what's possible, let's take a deeper dive now into each element of *The Transformational Giving Playbook*™.
~~~~

Guidance

The foundation for any significant change, must start with the Organization as a whole, and specifically, with the leadership within the organization. That's why the first component of *The Transformational Giving Playbook*™ is Guidance. Guidance focuses on what needs to happen at a leadership level to create a solid foundation for transformation. In the Guidance component of the playbook, we focus on three key elements—Transformational Leadership, Transformational Goal Setting, and Transformational Values.

Transformational Leadership

The implementation of *The Transformational Giving Playbook*™ requires change on every level of the organization. It takes a special kind of leadership to effectively guide an organization through this kind of change.

A traditional approach to leadership is one that is transactional. This is what most of us experienced in school—we were told what was expected of us, and then we were "graded" on our performance. In organizations, this translates to leaders communicating what one must do to be rewarded, and the consequences that will occur if one does not perform satisfactorily. This "carrot and stick" style of leadership may be effective and even necessary, in some situations—like in the military or in a crisis situation, where everyone must know exactly what is required of them and how a task is to be performed under pressure; however, it is not well-suited for leading organizations and individuals through change.

For that, a transformational style of leadership is much more effective.

It was James MacGregor Burns who first conceptualized the idea of leadership as either transactional or transformational back in 1978. But it was Bernard Bass and Ronald Riggio who built on Burns' work and literally wrote the book on Transformational Leadership in 2006.

In it, Bass and Riggio outline key qualities of transformational leaders, which we've summarized here. They:

- **Stimulate and inspire** others to achieve more than they thought possible.
- **Help others grow and develop** their leadership capacity through coaching and mentorship.
- **Empower others** to pay attention to their individual needs and invest in personal development, knowing it helps develop their leadership potential.
- **Inspire others** to commit to a shared vision and goals for an organization.
- **Challenge others** to be innovative problem solvers.

The important thing to understand is that Transformational Leadership is a skill. And although some leaders may naturally lead in this way, for others, it can feel awkward and foreign at first, especially if we have been trained in a more transactional style of leadership and/or if most of our models of leadership have been transactional.

The good news is, just like any other skill, a transformational style of leadership can be learned.

Here are the experiences we've found valuable in developing a Transformational Leadership Skill Set. In addition, these experiences help create a common language and approach among the leaders of your organization so that everyone is on the same page.

Leadership Training

Leadership training provides a powerful interactive context in which to not only learn transformational leadership skills, but to practice and develop proficiency in a context that is safe and supportive.

Executive Retreats

Executive retreats create an immersion experience that fast tracks transformational leadership skill development. In addition, because Executive Retreats are often conducted away from the office, and typically with a small group of executives and/or board members, it provides a powerful context for connection and cohesion among the leadership team.

Breakthrough Performance Coaching

Coaching is based on the belief that the way we do anything is the way we do everything. Breakthrough Performance Coaching helps leaders gain greater awareness of the ways they tend to lead, interact with people, and move through life. With this greater sense of awareness (i.e., emotional intelligence), coaching then helps leaders develop and apply new skills and unlock their full potential as a transformational leader.

Case Study: Elizabeth Green

Co-Founder & CEO, Civic News Company

Everything coaching has brought has been exceptionally helpful. I am a better leader because of it.

When I first started coaching, I actually felt like I was doing fine as a leader. At best I thought I might have some blind spots, so I was open to the process. But coaching has given me the opportunity to take a closer look at myself and improve as a leader. It's helped me see the places I was scared to take action as a leader; it's helped me understand why I was scared; and it's given me the tools to change the beliefs that fed that fear, so that I can be a more effective leader.

Through coaching I've gained the courage and personal strength to be as bold as I need to be. But the bolder you are as a leader, the more likely people are to criticize or critique you, so I am grateful for the personal infrastructure coaching has given me to be okay with that and not let it stop me from making important decisions that need to be made, or having hard conversations that need to be had. I am now confident enough to hear feedback and take it in, and I am making decisions, and having hard conversations, more quickly and with greater confidence.

Because my results were so positive and powerful, I committed to offering coaching to our entire leadership team.

As a result, our performance review process this year was the best ever. Leading with curiosity about the areas in which someone can improve created a completely different conversation. One in which we are able to acknowledge that no one is perfect, but we're in active conversation with ourselves and each other about how we want to grow. As a result, we are more effective as a team, our team dynamic has gelled and my relationship with everyone is stronger.

At the end of the day, it is people who make decisions, people who lead teams, people who make strategic plans, people who ask for donations. We've realized that our decision to invest in our people through coaching is one of the most important investments we've ever made.

~~~~

Transformational Goal Setting

Typically, fundraising goals within an organization are set as a single target number, so that at the end of the fiscal year or the end of the
~~~~

fundraising campaign, you either hit the target or you don't. What this can set up for the fundraisers and the organization as a whole, is a feeling that either we won or we lost. What we've noticed is that sometimes these goals are so large, they seem "unrealistic," and fundraisers can feel defeated before they even start. On the other hand, to counter that, sometimes organizations will set very "realistic" goals that seem almost inevitable to hit, but at the same time, don't inspire the team to do more.

We recommend a different approach.

Transformational Goal Setting is an innovative approach to goal setting that will actually move the needle farther faster in your organization and ultimately help you transform your ability to make the impact you're here to make.

This is what enables your organization to go from ineffective goal setting that often feels boring and burdensome and doesn't move the needle far enough fast enough, to goal setting that inspires and empowers team members to reach farther than they thought they could and enables the organization to achieve much bigger bolder goals.

A quick look at the differences between the old (traditional) way of goal setting, vs the new (transformational) way of goal setting demonstrates why this is such a powerful approach.

Old Way	New Way
Transactional (being **graded**)	Transformational (being **inspired**)
Appeals to **fears**	Appeals to **dreams**
Held over us	Calls us **higher**
Aims for what seems **possible**	Aims for what seems **impossible**
Sure shot	**Moonshot**
Checkbox exercise	**Creative** Exercise
Evaluates performance on things you **can't control**	**Distinguishes between what you can and can't control**, and evaluates performance on the things you can

Transformational Goal Setting uses a tiered approach, starting with the broad area of Focus and drilling down to the specific Tasks required to achieve each goal. This makes goal setting an exercise that is powerful, inspiring, and actionable.

Below are the six tiers of Transformational Goal Setting[2].

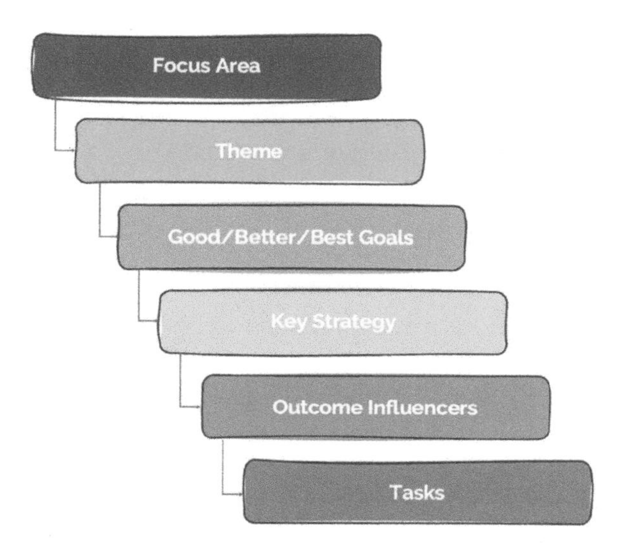

Focus Areas are the broad categories under which your organization establishes goals. Examples include Revenue, Impact, Growth, and Brand.

The **Theme** is intended to be an inspirational and visionary statement, versus measurable. Themes are intended to be a rallying call behind which your staff can unite and come together. The Theme can be for one fiscal year or run across years.

Good/Better/Best (GBB) Goals provide targets that inspire your team to rally around not just one specific target, but rather a range of targets. **The Good goal** represents what you "can live with." Often this reflects your budget numbers. **The Better goal** represents the number you'd really like to hit. The one that inspires the team to go the extra mile and achieve something everyone is proud of. **The Best goal** is where the magic happens. This is your moonshot. This is where organizational leaders and team members alike come together to think outside the box, to think bigger, to think better, and to act bolder than they ever have before. This is where we invite you to ask…

"What would you do if you didn't believe it was impossible?"

This is where the greatest achievements can be won and the greatest legacies can be created. GBB goals are **measurable but NOT controllable**. And once you set them, they are set; they are **not to be changed**. GBB goals should at least be set annually, and it can be helpful to break them into quarterly goals as well, depending on the nature of the goal.

The **Key Strategy** is just that, the primary strategy, or approach, you'll use to achieve the GBB goal. There are many ways in which a goal can be achieved, so the Key Strategy helps narrow the focus. This is not meant to be measurable, but rather a description of what you'll focus on in order to achieve the goal.

Outcome Influencers are exciting, because they are what **make the goal inevitable**. Outcome Influencers describe those **things you will increase or improve** in order to achieve or exceed the goal. Think of Outcome Influencers as the plan. Typically, there are multiple Outcome Influencers per GBB Goal. Outcome Influencers are **measurable and completely controllable**, and they are intended to be **nimble and changeable**. In other words, if they are not working to keep you on track toward achieving the GBB goal, then you should find a new way, adjust, retool, and even abandon the current plan in favor of a plan that will work. This is why you want to review Outcome Influencers, and adjust if necessary, at least once a month.

Tasks are **how you execute on the Outcome Influencers**. Achieving the goal is ultimately all about the execution. The Tasks indicate the What, Who, and When: What's the action that needs to happen? Who will do it? and by When? Tasks are **completely measurable and controllable**. They are best divided up into two- to four-week sprints. This keeps the team focused on the next right actions to take and helps prevent a sense of overwhelm.

Below is an example of what the Transformational Goal Setting approach looks in action. We've provided one GBB goal along with two sets of Outcome Influencers and Tasks for that goal; however, your organization is likely to have several goals for a given fiscal year (one annual revenue goal and several non-revenue goals) and two or more Outcome Influencers for each goal.

Focus Area: Revenue

Theme: Exponentially grow our revenue through a focus on transformational gifts of $100K+.

Annual GBB Goal: Increase the number of qualified prospects within the transformational gifts pipeline to 75%/85%/90% by the end of Q3.

Key Strategy: Streamline the prospect research and qualification process.

Q1, Outcome Influencer #1: Improve the tracking system for tracking when exploratory conversations are completed in relation to when prospects are assigned.

Tasks:

1. Submit a request to Development Operations for a Qualification Status Report, filterable by Relationship Manager.
2. Create the Qualification Status Report to identify when potential prospects are assigned to a Relationship Manager portfolio and when the exploratory conversation is conducte.
3. Test the Qualification Status Report.
4. Iterate on the Qualification Status Report.
5. Train staff on how to properly record exploratory conversations.

Q1, Outcome Influencer #2: Increase the number of exploratory conversations completed within 6 weeks to 100%.

Tasks:

1. Run a Qualification Status Report to understand the current completion time between portfolio assignment and exploratory conversation.
2. Provide each fundraiser with a baseline report of their completion times and an average completion time.
3. Provide mentorship on strategies for securing a meeting.
4. Provide fundraisers with monthly Qualification Status Reports to understand their progression.

Note: Each task would have a person assigned to it and a date by which it should be completed.

To download a template to assist you in the Transformational Goal Setting process, go to:

transformationalgivingplaybook.com/TGPtemplates.

"Until you can imagine it, you can't do it."

"Transformational Goal Setting ***helped us imagine the possibilities****. Just the activity of putting together* ***Good/Better/Best goals was transformational****. But the Outcome Influencers helped us operationalize success and gave people confidence by giving them the tangible things they could focus on to move the needle forward."*

~ Amy Kwas, VP of Development
The Children's Museum of Indianapolis

Transformational Principles

As a beginning step in the implementation of *The Transformational Giving Playbook*™, we recommend key leaders and team members gather together to create Guiding Principles for Fundraising. These Principles create a framework for healthy relationships inside and outside the organization and provide the basis for smart decisions around investment options. Additionally, if you do not already have them in place, you may want to identify your core values as an organization. Once you define your Guiding Principles for Fundraising—in alignment with your organization's core values—we recommend you publish and distribute them to all staff and display them in public areas in the office. They serve to create a shared sense of purpose, connection, and direction within the organization, which is essential to the organization moving forward, as one, to raise more money and do more good.

Case Study: Share Our Strength

Share Our Strength developed a set of Guiding Principles to frame how they approach fundraising activities and operations. The Guiding Principles direct how Development staff operate individually and within teams, how they collaboratively work with and support other teams, and how they engage with the organization's prospects, donors, partners, and other constituents. Moreover, these principles reflect and align with Share Our Strength's organizational core values, which every staff person shares, lives, and breathes in their day-to-day work.

Share Our Strength Core Values

A. BE BOLD
We have a clear mission and ambitious goals.
Think big. Be Fearless. Remember: we make the rules.

B. MOBILIZE STRENGTHS
Everyone has a strength to share.
Make connections. Bring people in. And show others how to support our mission.

C. DEMAND DIVERSITY
Diverse thinking creates stronger solutions.
Inclusivity isn't optional. Commit to diversity of ideas, people and communities.

D. DRIVE INNOVATION
We need to keep the entrepreneurial spirit alive.
Be inventive. Try new things. Challenge the status quo.

E. INSPIRE FUN
Fun isn't frivolous; it's key to our success.
Do good work and have a good time while you're at it. Encourage passion in others.

Share Our Strength Fundraising Guiding Principles (Summary Version)

1. LEVERAGE BEST PRACTICES (A,B,C,D,E)
Adopt industry best practices in relationship management, while allowing flexibility for departmental differences.

2. BUILD INSTITUTIONAL MEMORY (B,C,E)
Permanently capture constituent data in one place to help coordinate relationship building across individuals and teams.

3. ACHIEVE ORGANIZATIONAL GOALS (A,B,C,E)
Actively support one another in achieving individual, team, and broader organizational goals.

4. INTEGRATE RELATIONSHIP MANAGEMENT (B,C,E)
Orchestrate multi-touchpoint constituent engagement efforts with the right players through a clear Relationship Manager.

5. MEASURE AND REWARD THE RIGHT THINGS (A,D)
Measure and reward teamwork, cultivation activities, and revenue results to maximize the lifetime value of constituents.

6. BE BOLD WITH THE ASK (A)
Our default approach should be to make our first Ask big and bold.

7. ACT WITH URGENCY (A,D)
Be thoughtful and strategic, yet opportunistic and impatient.

8. LIVE THE BRAND (A,B,C,E)
Develop your own personal story and connection to the mission.

9. MOBILIZE STRENGTHS OF CONSTITUENT NETWORKS (A,B,C,D,E)
Equip each constituent to spread the word and amplify our organization's impact.

Share Our Strength Detailed Guiding Principle Examples

Here are two examples of the level of detail we recommend when documenting your guiding principles:

BUILD INSTITUTIONAL MEMORY	Corresponding Core Values
Permanently capture consistuent data in one place to help coordinate relationship-building across individuals and teams.	B: Mobilizes strengths C: Demand Diversity E: Inspire Fun

Fundraising is most effective when the right hand knows what the left hand is doing, hence collaboration across departments and markets requires access and transparency to constituent data. Much like we expect our bank to understand the complete scope and transaction history of our account(s)—with whom we've engaged, and ultimately, our value to them—it should be easy for every Development staff person to function from a data-driven place by having ready access to the full picture of our constituents and their history of engagement. This means transparency must transcend individual conversations. We must capture all that we learn about and do with constituents in a central place—our CRM—to build institutional memory for Share Our Strength that lives beyond any individual staff member.

LIVE THE BRAND	Corresponding Core Values
Develop your own personal story and connection to the mission.	A: Be Bold B: Mobilizes strengths C: Demand Diversity E: Inspire Fun

As fundraisers, it is our job to excite and inspire our constituents. Part of that is being able to tell our "story of me", along with other personal stories about the transformative impact of our work. When we demonstrate our passion for Share Our Strength's mission and values, coupled with infusing a spirit of hospitality into our fundraising, inspired by our long history of partnering with the restaurant industry, our passion and hospitality become contagious and spark the interests of constituents. People embrace our mission in big ways when we can effectively convey and speak enthusiastically about the work we do and how it changes the lives of real people within our communities.

~~~~
~~~~

Groundwork

The Groundwork component of the playbook is all about the nitty-gritty. This is where the hard but rewarding work of fundraising actually happens. The Groundwork component is focused on equipping frontline fundraisers with the Transformational System, the Transformational Skill Set and the Transformational Tools they need to succeed. That's why this part of The *Transformational Giving Playbook*™ ultimately transforms teams, as it equips everyone to be a winner.

Transformational System

"Moves Management" has been the traditional system used by major gift fundraisers (and some corporate and foundation fundraisers) since the 1970s. It's about initiating a series of actions to educate donors on the work of your organization to increase their commitment to the organization. It's about showing the donor how they can help the organization deliver on its mission.

Though the stages may seem similar, our Strategic Relationship Management Cycle goes beyond traditional Moves Management. It's about getting to know an individual, corporation, or foundation at the deepest level and helping them see how their support of your organization's mission can fulfill their motivations and aspirations. It's about showing how your organization can help, not only solve one of the world's greatest challenges, but can also help them create a legacy that gives their life deep meaning and purpose.

Up to this point when we've used the term "donor"; we haven't made a distinction between prospects who are brand new to the organization and existing donors. **As we break down each stage of the Strategic Relationship Management cycle, we'll use the term "prospect"**

for the first five stages of the cycle—regardless of whether the individual, corporation, or foundation has or has not previously donated to your organization—and use the term "donor" for the remaining stages.

The Strategic Relationship Management Cycle

The Strategic Relationship Management Cycle has eight stages, one of which applies only to corporations who enter into a fundraising agreement with your organization. Each stage has a clear purpose:

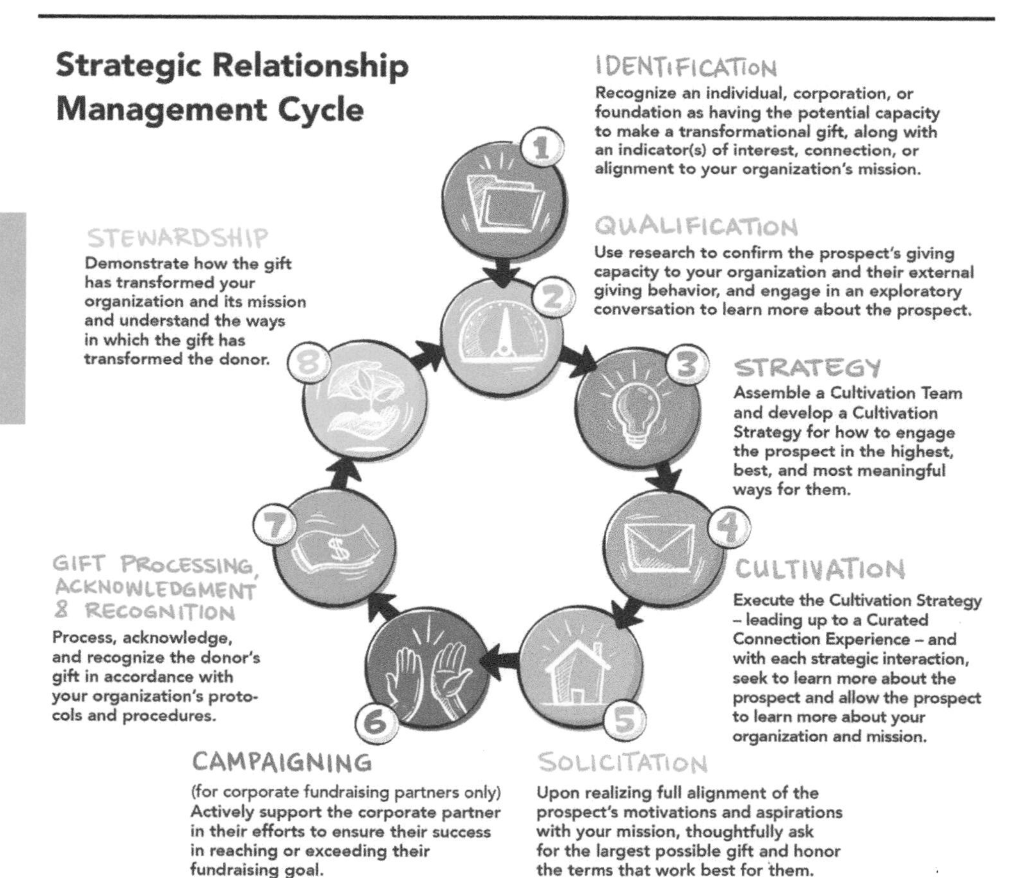

1. **Identification**. Recognize an individual, corporation, or foundation as having the potential capacity to make a

transformational gift, along with an indicator(s) of interest, connection, and/or alignment to your organization's mission.

2. **Qualification**. Use research to confirm the prospect's estimated giving capacity to your organization and their external giving behavior, and engage in an exploratory conversation to learn more about the prospect.

3. **Strategy**. Assemble a Cultivation Team and develop a Cultivation Strategy for how to engage the prospect in the highest, best, and most meaningful ways for them.

4. **Cultivation**. Execute the Cultivation Strategy—leading up to a Curated Connection Experience—and with each strategic interaction, seek to learn more about the prospect and allow the prospect to learn more about your organization and mission.

5. **Solicitation**. Upon realizing full alignment of the prospect's motivations and aspirations with your mission, thoughtfully ask for the largest possible gift and honor the terms that work best for them.

6. **Campaigning** (optional, for corporate fundraising partners only). Actively support the corporate partner in their efforts to ensure their success in reaching or exceeding their fundraising goal.

7. **Gift Processing, Acknowledgement & Recognition**. Process, acknowledge, and recognize the donor's gift in accordance with your organization's protocols and procedures.

8. **Stewardship**. Demonstrate how the gift has transformed your organization and its mission and understand the ways in which the gift has transformed the donor.

A few important things to know about the Strategic Relationship Management Cycle are:

- **It has no end.** Once a donor goes through the cycle the first time, the cycle starts again at the (re)Qualification or Strategy stage.

- **It is the same whether the prospect is an individual,**

corporation, or foundation, even though the specifics of the strategy and the investment of staff time may vary.

- **The duration of each cycle varies prospect to prospect**. For some prospects, alignment is achieved quickly; for others, it takes time. Prospects may also move forward and backward.
- **A prospect can be "unqualified" at any point during the first four stages**.
- **The cycle can be about more than a gift**. It could be about joining the board, sponsoring an event, supporting more than one location, or making multiple gifts[3].

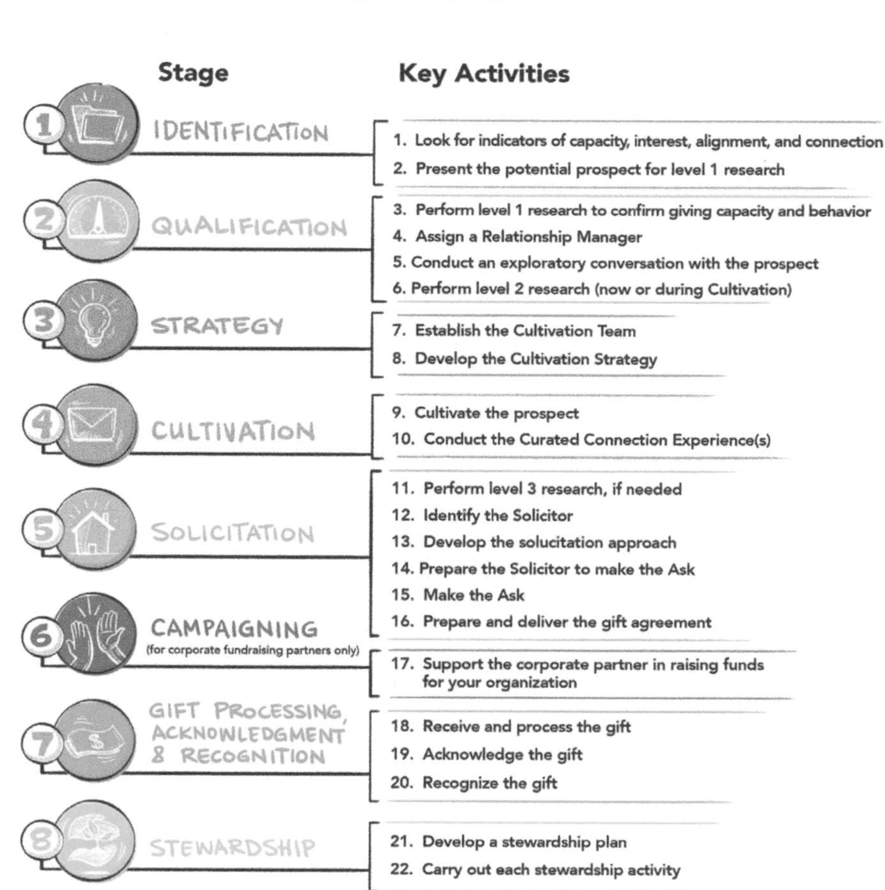

There are 22 activities that comprise the full Strategic Relationship Management Cycle.

Now for one more contextual note before we dive into more details about each activity. **Because this Playbook can be used by federated organizations, we use the terms "chapter" and "headquarters."** If your organization is federated, feel free to substitute chapters for affiliate, site, field office, regional office, or whatever term best describes the locally based offices that make up your organization. For headquarters, substitute worldwide office, central office, or the best term that describes the entity that constitutes your organization's center of operations.

Identification

Recognize an individual, corporation, or foundation as having the potential capacity to make a transformational gift, along with an indicator(s) of interest, connection, and/or alignment to your organization's mission.

A key to successful fundraising for transformational gifts is maintaining a strong pipeline of prospects. Prospects can come from a variety of sources, and these sources vary from organization to organization. Here is a reasonable starting list that your staff can use to think about what sources could be tapped to grow the prospect pipeline:

Referrals	Referrals from board members, staff, partners, and other donors
Personal Connections	Connections to potential prospects that staff members have
Top Lists	Philanthropists and philanthropic organizations that appear in national publications and local newspapers and business journals

Donors to Similar Nonprofits	Research you uncover about donors to other nonprofits with programs related to your mission
Donor Advised Fund Lists	Donors giving through giving vehicles through which they can make irrevocable, tax-deductible contributions that can be awarded, based on the non-binding recommendations of the donors, as grants to nonprofit organizations
Self-Identification	Individuals, corporations, and foundations who express interest in donating to your organization
Networking	People you meet at events where business groups and high-net-worth individuals gather
Event Attendees	People who attend events as a guest of an existing transformational gift donor
Prior Gifts	Prior gifts of a size, frequency, and/or longevity that suggest the capacity and/or inclination to make a larger gift
Wealth Screenings	Screenings performed on constituents within your CRM database
Past Prospects	Potential prospects in prior years for whom, at the time, there might not have been sufficient alignment of their motivations and aspirations with your mission

When you have identified and actively begun to tap your sources, it's time to kick off the Strategic Relationship Management Cycle for each prospect.

1. **Look for (additional) indicators of capacity, interest, alignment, and connection**
   The best transformational gift prospect for your organization is one who: has the **capacity** to make a transformational gift, has an **interest** in subjects that relate to your mission, is in intrinsic **alignment** with your mission, and has a **connection** to your organization through one or two degrees of separation or past engagement.

   When assessing capacity, interest, alignment and connection, be on alert for the indicators included in the Appendix. You are unlikely to identify many at this early stage in the Strategic Relationship Management Cycle, but a strong indicator of capacity and another indicator from the interest, alignment, or connection criterion may suggest you have a prospect for whom performing the next step, level 1 research, is prudent.

2. **Present the potential prospect for level 1 research**

   Staff and board members should use their best judgment to determine if a potential prospect warrants for research, based on whether at least one Capacity characteristic and at least one Alignment, Connection, or Interest characteristic are discovered. Prospects meeting these criteria should be submitted to your Prospect Researcher for level 1 research. Be sure to communicate any known information about the potential prospect (e.g., source of the prospect, contact information, biographical information, known connections, indicators of wealth, etc.) in your research request.

Qualification

Use research to confirm the prospect's estimated giving capacity to your organization and their external giving behavior, and engage in an exploratory conversation to learn more about the prospect.

3. Perform level 1 research to confirm giving capacity and behavior

The first phase of research, performed by a Prospect Researcher, involves confirming giving capacity and behavior. This represents a very streamlined approach to research—it should take no more than 15 minutes—because it is typically all that is required for the next step of assigning a Relationship Manager to conduct an exploratory conversation. Moreover, to do more research at this early stage has the potential influence the Relationship Manager too much, which could make the initial conversation with the prospect awkward.

The Prospect Researcher should review the cursory research data and determine two ratings based on the research data:

- **Estimated Giving Capacity Over 5 Years** - the amount the prospect is capable of giving *to your organization.*
- **External Giving Behavior** - the level of giving *to other charitable organizations.*

If the level 1 research results determine there is capacity to make a transformational gift to your organization, proceed to the next activity.

If transformational gift capacity is not confirmed, but an individual prospect is a public leader, industry leader, or philanthropist, the Prospect Researcher may still recommend proceeding; otherwise, the Prospect Researcher should update the status of the prospect record to "Unqualified," indicate the date, and specify the reason as "Exploratory Conversation." In addition, the Strategic Relationship Management Cycle record should be closed.

4. Assign a Relationship Manager

If a decision is made to actively pursue the prospect for a significant commitment, Prospect Research should determine the Relationship Manager for the prospect. We recommend this be done by Prospect Research staff because they are:

1. In an ideal position to make these determinations because they are familiar with the full list of transformational gift prospects,

2. Have an in depth understanding of your organization's rationale for how prospects are assigned to portfolios, often driven by factors such as:

   - **Scope** of Relationship Manager portfolios
   - **Geographic location** of the prospect
   - **Pre-existing relationships** between Relationship Managers and prospects
   - The **intake capacity** of Relationship Managers to absorb new prospects as determined by:

     a. The target size of their portfolio
     b. Distribution of prospects across the Strategic Relationship Management Cycle
     c. Phase of any fundraising campaign that might be underway

3. Closely aligned with Development staff in order to consult with others to make the best decision on behalf of the prospect.

5. Conduct an exploratory conversation with the prospect

The Relationship Manager is ideally responsible for conducting an exploratory conversation (otherwise known as a qualification or discovery call/meeting) with the prospect before any further actions are taken. It is important to do this even if you already know some of the answers to the questions proposed for this conversation because it is a way to **start building rapport** with the prospect. In instances where another staff member may have a pre-existing relationship with the prospect—as is often the case with senior leadership—there should be a thoughtful negotiation to determine the best person for this activity.

The purposes of the exploratory conversation are to a) begin to gather important **insights about the prospect, particularly their motivations and aspirations**, b) learn the prospect's **impressions of your organization**, and c) understand their **philanthropic**

interests to determine whether there is sufficient interest and potential alignment with your organization's mission to suggest they should be pursued for a transformational gift. It takes time to schedule these conversations, but you will save time in the long run by understanding where and with whom to prioritize your time.

Securing time on the prospect's calendar can be challenging, so it is important to leverage existing relationships to help you get that call. Consider leveraging:

- Board members who know the prospect
- Senior Leadership who knows the prospect
- Other transformational gift donors who know the prospect

When you are ready to conduct the exploratory conversation, in cases where you already know the prospect, the "lead-in" to the conversation should be to express appreciation for the ways in which they've been engaged with your organization (e.g., a recent gift or grant, event sponsorship, etc.). In cases where the prospect is brand new to your organization, the lead-in should be to gather feedback on some aspect of your programmatic work.

Exploratory conversations are best conducted in person; however, depending upon the size of your fundraising program, the prospect's availability, their location, and their preferred communication method, a phone call, or video meeting might be appropriate. Email is considered a last resort and should only be used if the prospect is unwilling to take a call or meeting. Relationship Managers should endeavor to **conduct an exploratory conversation within two to four weeks of the prospect having been assigned to their portfolio**.

The following list provides a short list of potential questions you might consider for an exploratory conversation to learn more about the prospect's *motivations, aspirations, impressions* and *philanthropic interests.* This list is not meant to be prescriptive or exhaustive; rather, it provides a starting point for the Relationship Manager to think about what type of questions would best enable them to determine if an individual, corporation, or foundation should be pursued or not pursued for a transformational gift. For additional guidance in planning for and conducting exploratory conversations, Relationship Managers should consult with the Prospect Researcher.

Motivations

- What draws you (or your organization) to this work?
- How did you (or your organization's leadership) become passionate about this cause?
- What are the things that motivate you in your life, your work, your giving?
- At the end of the day, what it is that gives your life meaning and purpose?
- At the end of the day, what societal problems do you want to play a role in solving?
- What would you say your WHY is—the thing that motivates you (or your employees) every day to do what you do?

Aspirations

- 1 year, 5 years, 10 years from now, what are some of the goals you want to achieve?
- What's the legacy you want to leave?
- What do you most want to be remembered for?
- What's on your bucket list?
- What is it that you would love to accomplish in your life?
- What is it that you would love to accomplish in relation to this cause?

Note: For examples of motivations and aspirations, please see the Gift section.

Impressions of Your Organization

- How familiar are you with our work?
- How familiar are you with the communities with whom we engage?
- What are your impressions of our organization?
- What aspects of our work do you find most compelling?

- How important is our organization to you / the company/the foundation you represent?
- Do you believe our organization is successful in ______________________________?
- In what ways do we need to evolve/expand/shift to make a bigger impact?

Philanthropic Interests

- What is important to you when deciding to support a nonprofit?
- With what other nonprofit organizations are you engaged? In what ways and why?
- How well does our work align with your philanthropic/social impact mission?
- Could you see yourself (or your company/foundation) becoming engaged with our organization? In what way(s)?
- Under the right circumstances, is our organization one you might consider supporting financially?

For family foundations, if there is not sufficient information available online to understand the scope of what the foundation funds, their funding priorities, etc., it may be necessary to obtain some of that information during an introductory call after which you would circle back to schedule an exploratory conversation. For introductory calls to family foundations, questions you might consider asking are:

- How are your funding priorities determined?
- How are your funding priorities and award decisions determined?
- What are your current funding priorities?
- How many funding cycles do you conduct each year?
- Do you grant unrestricted funds, restricted funds, or both?
- What size ($) grants do you generally award? By focus area?
- What is the general term of the grants you award - one-year, multi-year?
- What are the qualities you look for in potential grantees and in proposals?

- What is the process our organization would need to undergo to apply for funding?
- Are there reports or other requirements you would have of our organization, or what would you consider to be demonstrable evidence of your funding's impact?

6. Perform level 2 research (now or in Cultivation)

If the exploratory conversation goes well, the prospect moves from Potential to Qualified and the Relationship Manager should request the next level of research. There may be times when Relationship Manager decides to delay the next level of research until the prospect is in the Cultivation stage; however, **performing further research earlier in the Strategic Relationship Management Cycle can greatly inform who should be part of the prospect's Cultivation Team, which will collaboratively develop the Cultivation Strategy**. (More on this soon.) The counterargument is that the time it takes the Prospect Researcher to perform detailed research can delay Strategy and Cultivation efforts. This is a determination the Relationship Manager should make based on their best judgment.

The scope of level 2 research varies from organization to organization; however, generally speaking, it is likely to include:

Individuals

- Contact information
- Summary affiliations with your organization
- Biographical information
- Education
- Primary business affiliation
- Spouse business affiliation
- Summary asset values by asset type
- Philanthropic affiliations (e.g., board membership, event committees, other participation)
- Summary charitable giving or largest charitable gift
- Political affiliations
- Past giving to and engagement with your organization
- Known relationships that can be leveraged

Corporations

- Business overview and information about current business conditions
- Major markets
- Industry and business lines
- Key contacts
- Summary asset values, revenue information, and financial holdings
- Philanthropic interests
- Summary philanthropic giving
- Past giving to and engagement with your organization
- Known relationships that can be leveraged

Foundations

- History of foundation (origins, mission, giving areas)
- Key leadership (Board of Trustees, key staff)
- Funding programs
- Total assets
- Average grant amount
- Recent and relevant grants awards
- Allowable uses of grant funds (annual, capital, endowment, administrative costs)
- Summary philanthropic giving
- Grant application process
- Past giving to and engagement with your organization
- Known relationships that can be leveraged

Strategy

Assemble a Cultivation Team and develop a Cultivation Strategy for how to engage the donor in the highest, best, and most meaningful ways for them.

7. Establish the Cultivation Team

The first activity in the Strategy stage is for the Relationship Manager to establish a Cultivation Team for the prospect. Many nonprofits tend to function with Cultivation Teams of one (e.g., a Gift Officer), but that shortchanges the prospect. Cultivation Teams should be as broad and deep as necessary to allow any and all staff, board members, volunteers, and current donors who can contribute a valuable role toward achieving the best possible outcome for the prospect and your mission.

The Cultivation Team structure may vary based on your specific staffing configuration. Illustrated below is a basic model that can work for any nonprofit. You can find a graphical depiction of this basic structure and real-life client example within the Appendix.

- **Relationship Strategist** - if appropriate
  One or More Staff
  Serves as an advisor to the Relationship Manager in establishing the Cultivation Team, developing the Cultivation Strategy, and planning the Curated Connection Experience and solicitation approach for the prospect. This role is typically filled by a member of senior leadership.

- **Relationship Manager** - required
  One Staff Member
  Has overall accountability for the prospect and is responsible for strategically advancing the relationship by ensuring adherence to the Cultivation Strategy. Is also accountable for keeping the Cultivation Team engaged and informed. This role should always be filled by a fundraiser such as a Major Gift Officer, Corporate Partnerships Director, or Foundation Relations Director.

- **Natural Partner** - required, over time
  One or More Staff, Volunteers, or Donors
  Has a meaningful relationship with the prospect and insights into their motivations and aspirations. This relationship may predate your organization's introduction to the prospect, or it may develop naturally over time. A Natural Partner (i.e., a board member), may even make the Ask.

- **Program Partner** - required, over time
  One or More Staff
  Serves as the "content expert" by providing programmatic subject matter expertise to demonstrate alignment of the prospect's motivations and aspirations to the mission. This role is always fulfilled by a staff person with deep knowledge of your mission-based work.

A few things to note about this Cultivation Team structure:

1. The roles identified are not mutually exclusive; **one person may fill multiple roles.**
2. **The composition of the team may change** based upon new knowledge of the prospect's Interests, Alignment, and Connections; or internal staffing changes.
3. **The composition of the team may consist of multiple Development functions** (e.g., Major Gifts, Planned Gifts, Corporate Partnerships, Foundations, and Events) **and Program staff.**
4. For federated organizations, teams may be comprised of **a combination of chapter and headquarters' staff.**
5. **Roles may change over time** as your organization's relationship with the prospect evolves.
6. **Additional roles might be added** to the Cultivation Team Structure should your organization become larger and more complex over time.

8. Develop the Cultivation Strategy

Once the Cultivation Team for the prospect has been assembled, the next step is to develop a Cultivation Strategy for the prospect. The Cultivation Strategy should be developed before any cultivation activities take place with the prospect (outside of those normal to any pre-existing relationship the prospect has with your organization) to ensure the team approaches the prospect in the most thoughtful and appropriate way. If the prospect is brand new to your organization, the Cultivation Team will need to start out with more of a rough sketch than a full-blown strategy, and that's okay. Cultivation Strategies are meant to be fleshed out and more tightly adapted to the prospect over time.

Components of the Cultivation Strategy include:

- Understanding of the prospect
  - Motivations
  - Aspirations
  - General philanthropic interests
  - Giving interest areas specific to your organization
  - Known messaging that resonates with the prospect
  - Preferred method of consuming information

- Giving and Engagement Opportunities to Pursue
  - Target ask amount
  - Estimated ask date
  - Specific funding opportunities to pursue (which may involve multiple offices)
  - Engagement opportunities to pursue in addition to the gift (e.g., host/sponsor an event, join the Board)

- Planned, Strategic Cultivation Interactions
  - A set of *strategic* interactions (defined below) to be performed by members of the Cultivation Team and potential others

- Organizational Communications
  - A thoughtful review and determination of the organizational communications the prospect should receive while they are being cultivated for a transformational gift

With regards to prospect interactions, there is a difference between strategic interactions and passive interactions. For a cultivation interaction to count as **strategic**, it must:

- be tailored to the prospect,

- be (mostly) two-way, meaning, the prospect learns something new about your organization and your organization learns something new about the prospect,
- advance the strategy for the prospect, and
- establish further alignment of the prospect's motivations and aspirations with your organization's mission.

Examples of strategic interactions include:

- An exploratory conversation
- A phone conversation
- In-person or virtual meeting
- Conversation with senior leadership
- Cultivation event participation
- Curated connection experience (more on this soon)
- Proposal presentation
- Proposal submission*
- Letter of inquiry*
- Grant application submission*

*These are intentional exceptions to the "two-way" rule.

In contrast, passive cultivation interactions are one-way (the prospect learns something). Examples include:

- Mailing
- Voice mail
- Email
- Unplanned in-person contact
- Cultivation event invitation
- Meeting request

Passive interactions are important because they maintain the momentum with the prospect and lead to strategic interactions, but they are not the interactions on which Relationship Managers should be measured. Strategic interactions are what should count towards Relationship Manager goals and strategic interactions are what will be used to recognize "assists" by non-Development staff who participate in the Cultivation process.

Cultivation

Execute the Cultivation Strategy—leading up to a Curated Connection Experience—and with each strategic interaction, seek to learn more about the prospect and allow the prospect to learn more about your organization and mission.

9. Cultivate the prospect

Conducting Strategic Interactions
This stage is about carrying out the strategic interactions identified in the Cultivation Strategy. Cultivation Team members should consider these questions in advance of every strategic interaction:

- What is the best possible outcome for the prospect?
- What do you want to learn about the prospect?
- What do you want the prospect to learn about your mission?
- What questions do you think the prospect will have and how will you respond?
- How do you want the prospect to feel after the interaction?
- What will you ask of the prospect?

10. Conduct the Curated Connection Experience(s)

The Curated Connection Experience is the most critical strategic interaction of the Cultivation stage. The purpose of the Curated Connection Experience is to provide a carefully curated experience for the prospect that will impact them deeply with the importance of the mission and the people involved in the organization.

A Curated Connection Experience happens in-person, and generally comes in three flavors:

1. **The Connection-Ask Combo Meeting** that combines the Connection and the Ask in one meeting. For some people, time is even more valuable than money. For some people, time is even more valuable than money and they may only afford you one opportunity for a meeting. In this case, it is critical that you've prepared and worked through a comprehensive Cultivation Strategy with the Cultivation Team to know what

will constitute the most meaningful connection so the Ask is successful.

2. **The First-Time Meeting (most common)** where you meet the prospect for the first time to learn more about them, their motivations, their aspirations, their affinity for the mission, and the alignment of their motivations and aspirations to the mission.

3. **The Xth-Time Meeting** where you meet with the prospect multiple times.

For individuals, perhaps a first meeting with the prospect, then a second meeting with the prospect and their spouse.

For a corporation, the number of meetings is driven by what it takes to get to the ultimate decision-maker. You want to work with the primary contact to understand who's who within the organization (e.g., public affairs, government affairs, marketing, budget, etc.), then create a meeting strategy that gets you to the ultimate decision-maker.

For a foundation, you may or may not have an option for a meeting. For foundations that will take a meeting with you, focus your efforts on the Program Officer then expand into the broader circle of influence within the foundation as appropriate.

Use your understanding of the prospect, their motivations, aspirations, affinity for the mission, and the alignment of their motivations and aspirations to the mission, to create the best and most meaningful connection at this meeting. You do not want to move to the solicitation meeting until the prospect is ready.

In all of these meetings, the goal is the same: carefully and consciously curate an experience for the prospect that wows them and is so impactful and aligned with who they are and the kind of difference they want to make, that they want to take the next step with your organization.

Preparation for the Curated Connection Experience

Elements of the Experience

If you can align the elements of the experience with the learning style and/or the preferences of the prospect, that is very helpful. For example, if what is important to the prospect is to hear about the impact of the mission, you may want to have someone there to share their testimony or have a video with testimonials and visuals of your work. If the financials are most important, you'll want to have the P&L. If it is important to the prospect to connect with the CEO or Chair of the Board, you'll want to make sure they are there. This information about the prospect can be ascertained perhaps by a Natural Partner who knows them well, by making an educated guess, or even by asking the prospect directly what is important to them to know and learn about the organization in this meeting.

Participants & Roles

You'll want to determine which members of the Cultivation Team should be in the Connection Meeting and what roles they will play. At a minimum, the Relationship Manager and most appropriate Natural Partner should participate. It should be determined ahead of time who should schedule the meeting, facilitate the meeting, greet the prospect on the day of the meeting, and even who will escort them to the meeting location.

Location

Ideally, the Curated Connection Experience takes place at a location where the donor can see the impact of your organization in person. If that is not possible, then strive to meet at a location in this order of preference—organizational office, prospect's home, prospect's office, video conference.

Logistics

Details matter. And when it comes to the details of this meeting, you want to leave no stone unturned. Create a seating chart (we recommend that the facilitator sit next to the prospect and the person speaking the most sit across from them), create name placards, provide beverages and possibly food, determine the length of the meeting, make sure all the equipment works and the slide deck and video have been tested and are queued up. **In addition and importantly, create a proposal outline that can be used to facilitate quick turnaround of a gift commitment letter or proposal should you receive a green light from the prospect.**

The Experience Itself

Although each Curated Connection Experience will be different based on the organization and the prospect, there are common elements that are the same.

You want to ...

- Show impact.
- Inspire.
- Educate.
- Motivate.
- Learn about the prospect.
- Ask key questions.
- Be prepared with possible next steps.
- Be prepared to ASK FOR A MEETING to present a proposal for the highest and most meaningful way the prospect's philanthropy can advance the mission.
- Be prepared to ASK FOR A GIFT if the opportunity presents itself and have a draft gift commitment letter or proposal ready that can be tweaked and issued quickly.

Outcomes of and Follow Up to the Curated Connection Experience

There are three basic outcomes for the Curated Connection Experience, each of which requires a different follow-up strategy.

Green Light

This is the best possible outcome, when the prospect indicates that they would like to make a gift and maybe even suggests the amount they would like to give. In this case, you'll want to thank the donor for their desire to support the mission, summarize the things the donor has agreed to, and indicate that you'll send them a gift commitment letter, contract, or proposal within 48 hours (or whatever time frame is appropriate given the complexity of the solicitation).

The gift commitment letter, contract, or proposal should include a range of philanthropic options and should indicate the impact and recognition for each level of giving.

Yellow Light

In this case, the prospect isn't ready to commit yet, so you'll need to take a series of next steps to address questions the prospect may have, which may include preparing a proposal that documents how their philanthropy can make a difference and/or scheduling additional Curated Connection Experiences for their spouse, business partners, etc.

Red Light

In this case, the prospect indicates this does not feel like the right fit or right time for them to make a transformational gift to the organization. In this case, you want to thank them for their time and ask for permission to keep them apprised of what the organization is up to and perhaps reconnect at a later date.

You can download a Curated Connection Experience Blueprint and a Curated Connection Experience Planning Template at.

Telling a Transformational Story

A Cultivation Team member interacting with a prospect should be prepared to share a Transformational Story. This is a story about either your connection to the mission and how it has impacted your life, or a story of how you've borne witness to the impact of the mission on the lives of others. Your story could be as short as 3 minutes or as long as 30 minutes.

Your Transformational Story is meant to inspire the listener(s) to take action. There is a big difference between telling an inspirational story and telling a story that inspires action.

Crafting a clear, concise, and compelling story about why you are so passionate about your organization's cause, and/or how the organization changed your life or the lives of others, is an incredibly powerful component to the cultivation process.

The formula we have found particularly helpful for crafting this type of Transformational Story is the Hook, Book, Look, Took formula[4].

- **Hook** - Grab attention in a way that piques curiosity and makes the listener want to lean in and hear more.
- **Book** - Tell your story and make your point. What's the key lesson you learned, transformation you experienced or insight you gained?
- **Look** - Invite the listener to reflect on their own life or to "look around" at the current situation in a way that invites them to either a greater insight, or perhaps even a personal "ah ha" moment.
- **Took** - Invite the listener to take action. Don't be afraid to call people to something big and bold. Remember, the action they take has the potential to be transformative for them.

The key here is to understand that people connect through stories because, to one extent or another, we see ourselves in someone else's story. Donors give when they feel a connection, not only to the cause, but to the people involved in the cause. Let your story speak.

Here are a few more tips for crafting a powerful Transformational Story.

1. **Share the struggle** - Sharing the struggle connects us to our audience and sharing the transformation lifts them up and gives them hope that they can do it too.

2. **Never tell a story without a point and never make a point without a story** - Stories give the listener a powerful, visual way to connect to the point.

3. **Make your story UNFORGETTABLE** (not just memorable) - You do that by painting a picture so vivid that your audience can't get it out of their mind, heart, body, and soul. Share the details. Take us there.

4. **Never show the "scaffolding"** - i.e. Don't tell the background to preparing for the presentation—just tell the story. For example, don't say, "While I was preparing for this talk, I ran across a quote that really inspired me and I want to share it with you and hopefully it will inspire you too." [We've all heard this before.]

If you'd like to **download a template to help craft your Transformational Story, you can do so at:**

transformationalgivingplaybook.com/TGPtemplates.

Case Study: Cece's Story

Cece is a donor to The Children's Museum of Indianapolis. She shared her story (Hook, Book) with a Gift Officer and we've extended it (Look, Took) to show how Cece can tell that same story to other people she knows that might encourage them to give.

[Hook]

An important aspect to me of The Children's Museum of Indianapolis is the main stairs. It is one reason our family is so passionate about being donors.

[Book]

My second daughter was born with many medical issues.

She had six major surgeries within her first six months, was on continuous oxygen for the entire first year, had three open heart surgeries before the age of three, and was fed through a feeding tube until she was three and a half.

The doctors were uncertain if she would ever be able to sit up, talk, or walk.

But with 5–6 therapies a week she received at home, she was able to make continuous progress.

The Children's Museum also became a very important part of her therapy.

I believe that all children should be able to enjoy The Children's Museum of Indianapolis.

I brought my two daughters to The Children's Museum twice a week. My second daughter's favorite part of the museum was the carousel. The staff would allow her to ride it over and over again—even though it required bending the rules! The Museum helps all children learn and grow, but it is also an essential place in our community where all children can play and explore.

But I have very strong memories of the stairs.

The main stairs have a very small rise and a very long run, which made it possible for my daughter to learn how to go up and down stairs. She was very petite. And so, for some therapy sessions we met her physical therapist there. She was able to teach my child to climb up and down those stairs, and in the process, she gained both strength and confidence.

[Look]

The beautiful thing is that The Children's Museum of Indianapolis provides a safe and supportive environment for all children to gain strength and confidence.

For my child, important places included the stairs and the carousel.

But for other children, it may be seeing for the first time who they can become—an archeologist, artist, astronaut, human rights advocate, scientist, world traveler—and trying on those possible futures that gives them strength and confidence.

I'm happy to report that my daughter has graduated from high school and is now a sophomore in college.

[Took]

As you consider your support for The Children's Museum, I want you to know that it is so much more than a beautiful building with interactive exhibits and interesting experiences. It is an inclusive environment that gives kids the permission and confidence to be who they are and become anything and anyone they desire.

~~~~

Solicitation

Upon realizing full alignment of the donor's motivations and aspirations with your mission, thoughtfully ask for the largest possible gift and honor the terms that work best for them.

11. Perform level 3 research, if needed

When alignment has been achieved and the prospect is ready to commit, it is time to prepare for the Ask. The first step is to conduct any additional research needed to confirm the Ask Amount and inform the Ask Strategy. The Relationship Manager should determine what's needed and make this request of the Prospect Researcher.Additional research gathered in this activity by the Prospect Researcher are likely to include more details behind the summary information gathered in level 2 research. Using individuals as an example, that means discovering detailed past employment and compensation history, detailed assets, detailed charitable giving, etc. It could also include new information the Relationship Manager may want to understand, such as more in-depth information about prospect's family members and specific information about members of the prospect's personal network.
~~~~

12. Identify the Solicitor

The next step is to determine who should serve as the Solicitor and who should accompany them for the Ask. Ideally, the Solicitor should be a Natural Partner who has made a transformational gift in the past—that is, someone who can speak to a transformational gift they made and the satisfaction they derived from having made the gift. Absent a suitable Natural Partner, the Solicitor could be a member of Senior Leadership or the Relationship Manager.

Accompanying the Solicitor should be a program staff person who is well versed in the mission work you will ask the prospect to support, and possibly the Relationship Manager if they are not serving in the role of Solicitor.

13. Develop the solicitation approach

Once it's clear who will solicit the prospect, it's time to work on the solicitation approach: the what, when, and how.

- The **what** refers to what you will ask the prospect to give and potentially do.
  - For gifts, you'll want to be specific about the type of gift (outright gift, multi-year pledge, planned gift), the payment method as appropriate, and the timeframe of the gift (over what time period are you asking it to be paid?).
  - For engagement opportunities, you'll want to be specific about the service you wish them to provide or the role you wish them to play (board member, event sponsor) and the accompanying responsibilities of that role, and the timeframe of the commitment (when does it start and when will it end?).
- The **when** refers to the specific date on which you will make the Ask.
- The **how** refers to the specific method of the Ask. It is a:
  - Proposal submission
  - Solicitation letter
  - Solicitation meeting

14. Prepare the Solicitor to make the Ask

Making a successful Ask is very much a combination of art and science. It requires imagination and creativity, as well as a well thought out plan based on proven techniques and lots of practice.

When the time has arrived to make the Ask, the Relationship Manager should develop the solicitation approach in consultation with the Cultivation Team (particularly the Relationship Strategist), then coach the Solicitor. The Solicitor is ready when they are:

- knowledgeable about the prospect and their relationship to your organization,
- knowledgeable about the prospect's intrinsic motivations and aspirations and how they align to the organization's mission,
- well-practiced in delivering the Ask Script,
- clear on the amount to ask for and any other requests,
- prepared to communicate how the gift will transform your organization,
- prepared to communicate how the gift will enable the prospect to fulfill their ambitions, goals, dreams, and legacy (because the giver will be transformed too!),
- prepared to make the case for relevancy and urgency,
- prepared to share the story of their gift and the satisfaction derived,
- equipped with answers to potential objections, and
- prepared with possible next steps should the prospect say yes!

You can download a Solicitation Meeting Blueprint and Solicitation Meeting Planning Template at:

transformationalgivingplaybook.com/TGPtemplates

15. Make the Ask

The preferable way to make an Ask for a transformational gift is in person. Of course, if you are dealing with a prospect that will only accept written solicitations, then honor their request with a formal proposal or letter.

If your plan is to conduct a meeting …

- **Be Clear**. When you request a meeting with the prospect, be transparent in your reason. Say it's to ask for a gift because no one likes to be caught off guard.
- **Be Prepared**. When the Solicitor and program staff member arrive, the Solicitor should open the meeting with conversation that serves to put the prospect at ease, then move into the Ask script. At some point, the prospect may have questions about what you're asking them to fund and that is where the program staff member comes in. They can answer those questions so the Solicitor can be focused on the Ask.
- **Be Flexible**. No matter how prepared both people are, it is still important to be flexible. At the end of the day, the aim is to align your organization's mission to the intrinsic motivations and aspirations of the prospect, so Solicitors should return to that when in doubt.

That said, there are three possible outcomes to any Solicitation Meeting.

Green Light

"YES!" The prospect agrees to give at the level asked. In this case, thank the prospect for their commitment, underscore the impact their gift will have, and indicate you will follow up within 48 hours with documents to formalize their commitment.

Yellow Light

"Not yet." The prospect is not ready to say yes yet. To understand what is standing in the way, you can ask a simple question like, "Under what circumstances would you consider making a gift of that size, or potentially something different?" Typically, their response will fall into one of four categories.

- Change in terms - The prospect wants to change something about the gift: the timeline, the amount, the giving vehicles, the recognition rights. If possible, negotiate these changes in the meeting and close the gift or set a date and time to reconnect within 48 hours.
- More due diligence - The prospect wants to do more research and talk with more people. In this case, set an exact date and time to discuss and/or schedule these next steps.
- Need to think about it - Ask the prospect how much time they feel they need to think about it and set an exact date and time to reconnect with them.
- Have more questions - The prospect has questions other people need to answer. In this case, make a plan with the appropriate staff to get answers to the questions and set an exact date and time to reconnect with the prospect.

Red Light

"No for now." If the vetting, preparation, Curated Cultivation Experience, and Proposal have gone well, it is unlikely the prospect will say no at this stage; however, if they do, you always want to keep the door open. You might respond by saying, "Thank you for your time. With your permission, I'll keep you apprised of what we're up to at the organization, and perhaps down the line we can reconnect."

16. Prepare and deliver the gift agreement

When you reach this activity in the Strategic Relationship Management Cycle it means the prospect has agreed to making a gift! The final activity of the Solicitation stage is to prepare, deliver, and, if appropriate, negotiate, the commitment agreement. Examples of agreements include Pledge Commitment Letters, Memorandums of Understanding, Letters of Intent, Corporate Fundraising Agreements, and Cause Marketing Agreements.

Case Study: The Children's Museum of Indianapolis

Amy Kwas, VP of Development, The Children's Museum of Indianapolis

We had one particular win in the Corporate department that was exciting because we made a much larger ask than we had in the past and it enabled us to hit the "Better" goal for our corporate fundraising this year.

We had an organization that had given us $25K, but rather than just asking them to renew at the same level, this year we built a cultivation team, developed a clear cultivation strategy, did the research to determine what their giving capacity really was, and through our strategic interactions, we asked questions and listened, which enabled us to better understand their motivations, aspirations and what they were really looking for.

With all of that information, and with the right people together with the right ideas to create the right proposal, we used the Good/Better/Best framework to set our targets for the Ask. We then put together a custom Curated Connection Experience that spoke directly to the impact they were looking to have, presented our proposal, and they decided to contribute at the highest level of our Ask. So they went from $25K to $180K, which also enabled us to close the year with the highest revenue ever for our Corporate fundraising department.

~~~~

Campaigning (for corporate partners only)

Actively support the corporate partner in their efforts to ensure their success in reaching or exceeding their fundraising goal.
~~~~

17. **Support the corporate partner in raising funds for your organization**

The Campaigning stage is where the Relationship Manager and other staff provide active, ongoing support to a corporate fundraising partner so they can meet or exceed their fundraising goal for your organization and accomplish their business objectives. How nonprofits go about providing that support is very much dependent on the:

- Industry sector/corporate focus: retail, construction, entertainment, etc.
- Corporate infrastructure: culture, staffing, etc.
- Fundraising arrangement: donations made at the register, donation of a percentage of profit, a workplace giving campaign, etc.

Be prepared to actively support the corporate partner and conduct regular meetings to:

- Review their fundraising progress to date,
- Determine if they are experiencing any challenges with their fundraising campaign and what might be underlying those challenges,
- Offer suggestions to maximize their success,
- Identify any issues that might impact your ongoing partnership with the corporation, such as staffing changes, unmet goals of the corporation for the partnership, change in philanthropic focus, etc., and
- Agree on next steps.

Gift Processing, Acknowledgment & Recognition

Process, acknowledge, and recognize the donor's gift in accordance with your organization's protocols and procedures.

18. Receive and process the gift

When the gift is received, immediately set processing in motion in accordance with your organization's policies and procedures. Your organization is likely to have a gift transmittal form or coding procedures to ensure the gift is allocated appropriately within your CRM and financial systems.

19. Acknowledge the gift

Acknowledging a transformational gift is a team effort. A donor who makes a gift at this level should be thanked by multiple people (Chief Executive Officer, Chief Development Officer, a board member) and in multiple ways (phone calls, letters, handwritten notes), including a custom treatment. For example, a nonprofit involved in K-12 education, might create a custom video of teachers, staff, and students honoring the donor. Going this extra mile demonstrates how much you value the donor and makes them feel appreciated and special. It's also one of the ways we distinguish ourselves from other nonprofits they may support.

We recommend you create a Transformational Gift Acknowledgement Protocol for your organization that spells out: Who does What, When. There are no hard and fast rules; however, a few important guidelines are:

- Make the first verbal acknowledgement within 24 hours.
- Mail the first written acknowledgement within 48 to 72 hours.
- Thank the donor for any other commitments they made in addition to the gift.
- Deliver a unique, highly personalized treatment within 2 weeks.
- Engage senior leaders and board members in the acknowledgement process.
- Thank non-staff Natural Partners (board members, other donors) for their efforts in securing the gift.

Here is an example acknowledgement protocol to stimulate your thinking:

Timing	Method	Person Responsible	$100K to $499K	$500K to $999K	$1 Million+
Donor Acknowledgement					
2 to 4 hours	Phone Call	Chief Development Officer	Required	Required	Required
24 hours	Phone Call	Chief Development Officer	Required	Required	Required
48 hours	Phone Call	Chief Executive Officer	Optional	Optional	Required
1 week	Personalized Letter	Relationship Manager	Required	Required	
1 week	Letter from Board Chair	Relationship Manager			Required
4 weeks	Official Tax Receipt	Development Operations	Required	Required	Required
Natural Partner Acknowledgement					
1 week	Phone Call	Relationship Manager	Required		
1 week	Phone Call	Chief Development Officer		Required	
1 week	Phone Call	Chief Executive Officer			Required

20. Recognize the gift

Assuming the donor has not requested their gift remain anonymous, your organization should recognize the gift in all the standard vehicles like the annual report, gala programs and presentations, and wall plaques.

But there's more. Similar to how you acknowledge the gift, you want to create unique recognition opportunities the donor can't get at any other organization. It matters to donors that they are valued and appreciated. It matters that they feel they are special to your organization. The way you recognize them plays an important role and sets the foundation for the next phase of the cycle—Stewardship—the timing of which overlaps with this activity.

Key questions Cultivation Teams should consider in creating a unique recognition opportunity for a donor are:

- Would the donor want to be recognized privately or publicly?
- What recognition vehicles or venues (publications, website, branded gift, events, etc.) align to the donor's motivations and aspirations?
- By whom within your organization would the donor appreciate being recognized?
- What events are upcoming that would serve as a good recognition opportunity?
- What permanent recognition opportunities are appropriate for the size of the gift (e.g., wall plaque, naming of a physical space, etc.)?

Stewardship

Demonstrate how the gift has transformed your organization and its mission and understand the ways in which the gift has transformed the donor.

21. Develop a stewardship plan

There is an important distinction between cultivation and stewardship: organizations **cultivate** *donors* and **steward** *gifts.* Therefore, stewardship plans include strategic interactions designed to demonstrate the positive impact of the gift and ensure the donor is deeply satisfied with having made it.

The Cultivation Team should begin work on the Stewardship Plan after all acknowledgements for the gift have been issued. Program Partners should be primarily responsible for carrying out the strategic stewardship interactions, while the Relationship Manager is accountable for ensuring they happen and are recorded in the CRM.

For a stewardship interaction to count as strategic, it must:

- Be **tailored** to the donor.
- Provide a **direct encounter** with the mission work they funded.

- Demonstrate **alignment** of the prospect's motivations and aspirations with your organization's mission.
- Instill **deep satisfaction** in the donor for having made the gift.

It's important to avoid the mistake of thinking regular, generic program communications (newsletters, save the date notices, annual report mailings, general program updates, etc.) and impromptu interactions constitute the whole of effective stewardship, or to think recognition of the gift equates to gift stewardship. **Fulfilling donor motivations and aspirations and instilling satisfaction are the goals of stewardship.** You want the donor feeling so good that it compels them to give again.

How you approach stewardship planning differs depending on whether the donor is an individual, corporation, or foundation, but the key interactions to consider in all stewardship plans are: special invitations, personalized or exclusive experiences, and personalized communications. With every strategic interaction you include, strive to make it:

1. **Unique** - something the donor can't experience anywhere else.
2. **Uplifting** - something that is engaging and fun.
3. **Inclusive** of the right people - involve people with whom the donor would like to develop or deepen a relationship.

The other important thing to note about stewardship plans is **the duration of the plan should match the duration of the gift**. That means you will steward an annual gift for one year, a five-year pledge for five years. For multi-year stewardship plans, be mindful to vary the experiences for the donor so they are new and different and serve to bond the donor more strongly to your mission.

22. Carry out each stewardship activity

This section is about carrying out the strategic interactions identified in the Stewardship Plan. Whoever is interacting with the donor should consider these questions in advance:

- What specific aspect of the mission do you want the donor to experience?

- What is the 'something new' you want them to learn about your organization's work?
- In what specific way will you convey how their gift is making a difference?
- What questions do you think the donor will have and how will you respond?
- How do you want the donor to feel after the interaction?

As mentioned early on in this section of the book, the Strategic Relationship Management Cycle has no end. At some point during the Stewardship stage—when the indicators of willingness to make the next transformational gift are strong and/or the donor's gift is no less than six months from being fully utilized—the Cultivation Team should begin a new relationship management cycle for the next transformational gift. Continuous momentum is essential to fulfilling the donor's motivations and aspirations and maximizing their support for your organization. This next cycle should begin at the Strategy stage or the (re)Qualification stage if it has been five years or more since the last gift was made.

Transformational Skill Set

The Transformational Skill Set component of *The Transformational Giving Playbook™* is based on the belief that success as a high-touch fundraiser does not require superstar talent that some have and some don't, but rather it requires a high-touch fundraising skill set that can be taught and learned. Moreover, we know that the better equipped one is to succeed, the greater the sense of joy and satisfaction one has in the work they do. Equipping staff with the skills to successfully contribute to the securing of transformational gifts is key to the success of the program and to the transformation of the teams. In this way, everyone is empowered to be a winner.

Mentorship

One of the most powerful methods for teaching this transformational skill set is by leveraging the fundraising superstars in your organization as mentors to the newer members of the team. A mentor is someone who has done it before. They've "climbed the mountain," and they've successfully secured significant gifts multiple times. Their experiential knowledge, innate talent, and real-life know-how are invaluable assets to the team and perfectly positions them to mentor others in those same skills.

The following is a classic four-step model of mentorship that works well with transformational gift fundraising.

1. **I do it.**

   The superstar fundraiser acquires multiple significant gifts.

2. **I do it, you watch … and ask questions.**

   The mentee accompanies the mentor on a face-to-face meeting and observes and asks questions. These could be actual interactions with the donor or meetings done via role-play. **The key skill here is to learn how the mentor THINKS, not just what they do.** What was their thinking behind changing the approach to the conversation from what was planned or behind bundling the Ask with additional opportunities for the donor? **Learning to THINK like a superstar fundraiser is the KEY.** When the mentor feels like it is time to nudge the mentee from the nest, they move to the next stage.

3. **You do it, I watch … and offer feedback.**

   The mentee conducts the face-to-face meeting while the mentor accompanies them. Again, this can be an actual interaction with the donor or done via role-play. The key here is for the mentor to offer feedback to the mentee on what they did well and areas where they can improve. Patience is key here for both the mentor and the mentee. Just like it takes a few tries to learn how to balance on a bike, it also takes practice to develop these skills and feel confident in them. But once the mentee reaches that stage, they are ready to move onto the next step.

4. **You do it.**

   The mentee is ready to interact with donors on their own and secure transformational gifts.

Training

In addition to mentorship, group training is also extremely valuable for helping build a Transformational Skill Set. Some of the training we believe is particularly helpful includes:

- **Strategic Questioning and Active Listening.** The best prospect research is done in person. Anytime you are face-to-face with a donor you are in the best position to learn valuable information about them. Fundraisers who know how to ask open questions, probing questions, and knowledge questions—and who are well-trained in how to listen—are incredibly effective at securing transformational gifts.

- **Crafting A Compelling Transformational Story.** It's incredibly powerful for fundraisers to craft their personal stories of why they are so passionate about your organization's cause and/or how the organization changed their lives and/or the lives of others. This is a key component of the cultivation conversations with any prospect or donor.

- **Effective Prospecting with the Board.** The most effective boards are those on which all members are willing to serve as some combination of an advisor, advocate, and fundraiser. For those willing to serve as fundraisers, it is important they are willing to open contact lists and doors, to lead by example (give, get), and to show up and participate fully. It takes time and skill to get board members to reveal their network and to assess their level of comfort with fundraising and what they are willing to do on your organization's behalf.

- **Facilitating Pipeline Meetings.** Transformational Giving Pipeline meetings are one of the most essential tools for your

Cultivation Team and facilitating them well is critical to the success of your Transformational Giving program. This is why we recommend specific training on their facilitation. (See more below in Transformational Tools.)

- **Ask Script Development.** No Ask Script is exactly the same, but typically the Ask takes place in the Solicitation Meeting after a proposal has been sent with a range of giving and impact options. The fundraiser making the Ask should be familiar with all aspects of the proposal, know exactly what the opening Ask is (the highest amount stated in the proposal), know exactly what outcomes and/or impact the donor should expect from their contribution, and know what terms and options can be negotiated to secure the gift.

Skill Building

Understanding HOW to do something is the first step toward developing a Transformational Skill Set, but it is the practicing of that skill that actually builds the "muscle memory" to perform that skill. That's where we have found role-playing is particularly helpful.

Here are some of the **skills we've found helpful to role-play**:

- The Exploratory Conversation
- Telling your Transformational Story
- Prospecting with Board Members
- Pipeline Meeting Facilitation
- The Solicitation Meeting

To help facilitate the building of these skills, we recommend developing scripts, blueprints and/or templates for each of these. We have created blueprints for each of these conversations, which you can download from our website at:

transformationalgivingplaybook.com/TGPtemplates.

Transformational Tools

A carpenter without a hammer, a drill, and a saw would have a hard time building a house—at least in an effective and efficient way. Putting the right tools in the right hands to perform the right tasks is critical to the success of the mission. The same is true with your Transformational Giving program. Equipping team members with the right tools to capture information about your transformational gift prospects, track your efforts throughout the Strategic Relationship Management Cycle, track your progress toward your GBB goals, Outcome Influencers, and Tasks, and effectively conduct Transformational Gift Pipeline Meetings, are just some of the tools that are critical to the success of your Transformational Giving program.

RACI Framework for the Strategic Relationship Management Cycle

To assist you in understanding who to involve in each activity of the Strategic Relationship Management Cycle, we have created a RACI table that identifies:

- Who is *Responsible* for performing the activity.
- Who is *Accountable* or "on the hook" for the outcome of the activity.
- Who should be *Consulted* for their opinion or asked to provide input.
- Who should be *Informed* of progress or of the activity's completion.

We use generic terms to describe the staff roles, which you'll want to modify to reflect the specific job titles used within your organization. The RACI table is available to download from our website at:

transformationalgivingplaybook.com/TGPtemplates.

Transformational Gifts Pipeline Meeting Framework

"Pipeline meetings are where all the magic happens."

~ Jeremy Cramer

Case Study: Jeremy Cramer,

Former VP of Major Gifts at City Year

During the time I was at City Year, we drove everything through our Pipeline Meetings. It's where the sausage was made. It was where all the components of The Playbook came together and it was critical to our fundraising success.

Specifically, the Pipeline Meeting contributed to our fundraising success in four key ways.

1. **Improved Donor Cultivation**
   Pipeline Meetings enabled us to do four things critical to the cultivation process:
   - Seek a diverse set of opinions on specific relationships.
   - Build consensus on targeted strategies for donors and prospects.
   - Hold each other accountable for the work that we agreed to in previous meetings.
   - Build a dynamic and inclusive environment where everybody's opinion matters.

2. **Incentivized Team Collaboration**
   The Pipeline Meetings were also really valuable in helping us move beyond the "my donor" mindset and see the value of collaboration.

   The best way to get buy-in for all the processes in a Pipeline Meeting is to demonstrate that everybody wins if they participate. What we did at City Year was to ensure that the "pie" got bigger and that the pieces of the pie went to more parties than they otherwise would have.

   When people were able to see the value of collaboration in helping their site revenue increase, as well as that of the national office, that's when everyone really bought in.

To demonstrate this, we found a donor to offer a challenge grant to every City Year office. The intention of the challenge grant was to offer matching funds for City Year sites to secure new major gifts of $10K or more. For every five $10K gifts they brought in, the site received an additional $50K match from the donor. This incentivized everyone to participate in the Pipeline Meetings, because they could see how much they'd benefit.

3. **Inspired Positive Comportment**
   City Year's then-CEO was one of our best fundraisers and a role model to everyone else, and we made sure to include him in our Pipeline Meetings. That incentivized and inspired everyone to do their best work. If the CEO was carving out several hours a week to make time for this, surely other staff and members of the leadership team could too.

4. **Increased Fundraising Capability**
   One of our working hypotheses at City Year was that volunteer leadership in partnership with staff would bring out the best in our fundraising capability. To that end, we identified as many corporate partners as we could, who lived and worked in City Year locations, who were experienced deal makers and for whom Pipeline Meetings were core to their business success. We then paired those partners with City Year sites. When the partners participated in the Pipeline Meetings it helped staff understand just how essential it was to adhere to the processes in order to achieve our fundraising goals.

~~~~

The Transformational Gifts Pipeline Meeting is one of the most important tools at your disposal. It's the outward expression of the Strategic Relationship Management Cycle, where collaboration across fundraisers, departments, and locations happens on a grand scale to align the prospect's motivations and aspirations to your mission.
~~~~

If you approach your Transformational Gifts Pipeline Meetings in this way, it changes everything.

On a bi-weekly or monthly basis (depending on what's right for your organization), we recommend you hold 2-hour Transformational Gifts Pipeline Meetings to review your top priority, active prospects (i.e., those in Strategy, Cultivation, and Solicitation). The idea of a "pipeline meeting" sounds simple, but at the transformational gift level, to do them right requires cross-organizational participation, careful preparation, and effective facilitation.

In addition to the Transformational Gifts Pipeline Meetings, Relationship Managers should plan to conduct Cultivation Team meetings focused on a specific donor or donors the Cultivation Team has in common, and to hold Portfolio Review Meetings with their supervisor to cover progress against their portfolio writ large.

Participation

Identifying who should participate depends on your organizational structure. Still, strive to **be inclusive**. Aim for collaboration across departments and, if applicable, locations, because there is always something new to be learned about the prospect and benefits to realize from groupthink around the Cultivation Strategy for your transformational gift prospects. There is no one-size-fits-all participation model, but below is an example of a participant structure for a non-federated nonprofit. In the Appendix we provide an example for a federated organization.

Example Transformational Gift Pipeline Meeting Participant List (for a Non-Federated Nonprofit)

Participants	Role	Responsibilities
Chief Development Officer (always) and the Chief Executive Officer (as needed, based on the prospects being discussed)	Strategic Advisors	Brings the organizational perspective of the executive team, provides strategic guidance to on Cultivation Strategy and solicitation approach, and ensures alignment of those strategies and approaches with the mission and organizational funding opportunities
Director of Prospect Development	Moderator	Determines what prospects will be discussed and sets the agenda for the meeting in consultation with the Chief Development Officer and Relationship Managers, and moderates the meeting to keep all participants on track with the agenda
Director of Prospect Development or a Prospect Researcher	Organizer	Schedules the pipeline meeting and disseminates the agenda, and reports beforehand
Relationship Managers (i.e., Gift Officers)	Facilitators	Facilitate the meeting discussion about each of their prospects and records changes to the Cultivation Team, Cultivation Strategy, and solicitation approach in the CRM
Program Partner(s) and Other staff (as appropriate, based on the prospects being discussed)	Contributors	Offers insights that further inform the alignment of programmatic work to the donor's motivations and aspirations, in addition to the Cultivation Strategy or solicitation approach

Meeting Objectives

The objectives of Transformational Gifts Pipeline Meetings should always be to:

1. Share recent cultivation and solicitation successes.
2. Briefly review fundraising progress against your GBB goals, Outcome Influencers, and Tasks.

3. Confirm, and discuss if needed, any active prospects in Solicitation.
4. Share/elicit important insights on prospects in Strategy and Cultivation and discuss other fundraising efforts that might have a bearing on Cultivation (e.g., work occurring with a corporation that might be relevant to cultivation of their CEO, upcoming cultivation dinners, or work happening in a region that might be of interest to a prospect who is co-located).
5. Become familiar with new prospects assigned to Relationship Managers since the last meeting.
6. Determine if any prospects need to be removed from active prospecting at this time.

Preparation

Facilitators

To prepare for a transformational gifts pipeline meeting, Relationship Managers should make sure all data about their prospects is updated in the CRM system at least seven days (one week) in advance of the meeting, as the Director of Prospect Development will rely on this to prepare the agenda for the meeting.

Moderator

Between four to six days before the meeting, the Moderator should determine which prospects should be covered and prepare the meeting agenda. Selection criteria for determining which prospects will be covered include:

- All prospects in Solicitation for a transformational gift.
- The best 3 to 5 prospects in Strategy or Cultivation based on a thoughtful assessment of Capacity, Interest, Alignment, Connection and other donor ratings, as well as the Ask Readiness rating for the Strategic Relationship Management Cycles underway.
- Brand new prospects that have entered the Strategy stage.

The agenda should allocate a specific amount of time to each prospect, as the following example illustrates. Agendas will vary meeting to meeting.

Timeframe			Topic	Facilitator
9:00	-	9:10	Recent cultivation and solicitation successes	Moderator
9:10	-	9:20	Review of fundraising progress against goals	Moderator
9:20	-	9:35	Top prospect/donor in Solicitation (15 minutes per prospect) •	Relationship Managers
9:35 9:55 10:15	- - -	9:55 10:15 10:35	Top 2-3 prospects and donors in Cultivation and those entering Strategy (20 minutes per prospect) • • •	Relationship Managers
10:35	-	10:45	New transformational gift prospect assignments	Moderator
10:45	-	10:55	Prospects and donors to be unqualified at this time	Moderator
10:55	-	11:00	Wrap up / quick announcements	Moderator

Pipeline Meeting Preparation Timeline

-7 Days

Facilitators

Ensure the CRM system is up-to-date for all prospects in your portfolio, in particular the Cultivation Team, all prospect ratings, and the components that make up the Cultivation Strategy:

- Understanding of the Prospect
- Giving and Engagement Opportunities to Pursue
- Cultivation Team
- Planned, Strategic Cultivation Interactions

-6 to -4 Days

Moderator

Determine, in consultation with the Chief Development Officer, the transformational gift prospects to be discussed in the pipeline meeting and prepare the meeting agenda.

-3 Days

Organizer

Distribute the agenda and the following reports to all meeting participants via email:

- Fundraising Progress Report
- Transformational Gift Pipeline Tracking Report
- Cultivation Strategy Report for each prospect being discussed

Pipeline Meeting

All Participants

Share success stories, learn where we are against goal, and engage in a robust and healthy discussion about the prospects up for discussion.

Organizer

Next, the Organizer should prepare the following reports/documents for the meeting:

- A fundraising progress report that indicates progress toward overall fundraising goals
- A transformational gift pipeline tracking report that provides key statistics on prospects by stage and forecasted revenue based on the pipeline
- A cultivation strategy report (or completed template) for each active prospect being reviewed

Once the reports/documents are reviewed and completeness of the content confirmed, three days in advance of the meeting the Organizer should send an email with the meeting agenda and reports/documents to the participants.

Facilitation

At the appropriate time on the agenda, each Relationship Manager will facilitate the discussion for their prospect(s). Relationship Managers should be deliberate in leading the discussion and in sticking to the established agenda. They should also be mindful of participants' time and restrict the Transformational Gifts Pipeline Meeting to robust discussions that can inform and advance the Cultivation Strategy as opposed to providing quick updates.

Examples of questions Facilitators might want to explore are:

- Based on the prospect's prior giving and research, have we identified the strategic, organizational priority(ies) that best align with their motivations and aspirations?

- What is the overall philanthropic narrative (the story) we should be shaping for this prospect with our organization?

- How can we be more creative in helping this corporation deliver on its CSR business objectives?

- Based on what we know of the prospect and their relationships through research and our goals for funding, do we have the right people assigned to the Cultivation Team?
- Based on what we know about the prospect and what we've seen in research, whom do we think should participate in the next or a future strategic cultivation interaction? (Please note that the Relationship Manager is not always the right person to carry out each interaction).
- Is the next planned, strategic cultivation interaction the right one? Is it the right time?
- What creative techniques can help us secure a(nother) meeting?
- What messages and stories do we think need to be shared with this prospect next time we see them? What would it be helpful for them to learn about our organization?
- What potential questions/objections will this prospect have during our next strategic interaction?
- What do you suggest the Cultivation Team consider in planning for a Curated Connection Experience?

As the discussion unfolds, **the Relationship Manager should document changes** in the CRM system for their prospect, and the Organizer should capture key notes for the meeting record.

Pipeline Meeting Principles

When conducting Transformational Gifts Pipeline Meetings, it is important that every participant bring their highest level of creativity to the table because creativity is what enables us to think big and act bold. But being creative can be risky. When we're being creative, we put ourselves in the position of offering new ideas, strategies, and approaches that haven't been tried before and aren't necessarily proven.

Consequently, it's important to keep a few principles in mind to make sure everyone is heard, every idea is explored, and we don't shy away from the natural and healthy tension that emerges when we explore and talk through different ways of cultivating transformational gift prospects.

1. Create a safe space

Pipeline meetings bring together individuals with different perspectives. Some bring an organizational strategy perspective, others fundraising, and others have unique insights into the prospect. It is important that Moderators create a meeting environment where everyone is respected as a valuable partner in this work and encouraged to share their ideas and perspective.

2. No idea is a bad idea

When it comes to Cultivation and Solicitation, no idea is a bad idea. This Playbook imparts the science of fundraising, and we expect meeting participants to bring the art by thinking big and creatively about the best way to evolve strategy, deepen the relationship with the prospect, and showcase alignment of their motivations and aspirations with your organization's mission. Ultimately, the Relationship Manager will need to decide on the next steps with a particular prospect, but all ideas are welcome to inform their thinking.

3. Embrace healthy tension

Not everyone will agree on where to take the Cultivation Strategy, or what the next strategic interaction should be, or how to approach solicitation. Healthy tension is a good thing, and we shouldn't shy away from it because that's what allows us to test out different scenarios and come to the best ideas as a team.

Periodic Review of Lower Priority Prospects

While it is important to maintain momentum with active, high-priority prospects, it is important not to lose sight of lower-priority prospects. Therefore, we recommend organizations consider adding quarterly meetings to review any medium to low priority prospects that have not been discussed within a Transformational Gifts Pipeline Meeting. These supplemental meetings can be used to help inform the upcoming year's fundraising goals.

Annual Review of "Unqualified" Prospects

As the Strategic Relationship Management Cycle unfolds, some prospects will be unqualified for pursuit of a transformational gift. In the third quarter each year, the Chief Development Officer and Director of Prospect Development should review the list of unqualified prospects and determine if any should be revisited next year or in a future year. This meeting can be used to inform the upcoming years' fundraising goals.

CRM and Supplemental Tools

In an ideal world, your CRM system would track and report on everything we described in the Strategic Relationship Management Cycle. But, most CRM systems can't—not even the most ubiquitous ones. Part of what our team is looking to do next is work with software vendors to make the information you need to capture easy to do and, importantly, easy to report on. Until then, we've documented what your organization can do to configure your current CRM—even if it involves creative workarounds. For data that is likely to be difficult or unwieldy to track in many CRM systems, we have provided Word and Excel templates you can use at:

transformationalgivingplaybook.com/TGPtemplates.

CRM Configuration Guidelines

Understanding of the Prospect

Central to *The Transformational Giving Playbook*™ is understanding the prospect's motivations and aspirations so you can align them to your organization's mission. Consequently, Motivations and Aspirations should be narrative fields tracked on the prospect's record. They should appear in a place that is front and center when accessing the donor's record and they should be reportable. In addition to this, we recommend creating fields to capture other important information such as: General Philanthropic Interests, Giving Interests specific to your organization, Known Messaging that Resonates with the Prospect, and the Prospect's Preferred Means of Consuming Information.

Cycle, Stage, and Activity

Every Strategic Relationship Management Cycle that a prospect progresses through should be tracked within the CRM. Some CRMs have records called 'opportunity' or 'proposal' or 'plan' that can be used for this purpose. And, there will usually be a field that can capture the Stage of the cycle a donor is in (e.g., Identification, Qualification, Strategy, etc.). What is more challenging, and therefore might require some creative workarounds, is to track the specific Activity the prospect is in within a given Stage. Most CRM systems do not capture this level of detail, but there may be a field on the cycle record where you can store this data if that level of granularity is desirable.

If possible, you also track the start and end dates associated with the Cycle, each Stage, and each Activity. This will allow you to uncover trends that can inform future fundraising efforts.

Gift and Engagement Opportunity Tracking

The next important tracking components of the Strategic Relationship Management Cycle are the gift and engagement pursuits (plural) that make up the Cycle. For example, a federated organization might pursue a prospect for two annual gifts (e.g., one for the NY chapter and another for the FL chapter), in addition to a capital campaign gift; and you might ask the prospect to join the Board of Directors.

It's important to capture all the pursuits that fall under one cycle; however, the majority of CRM systems used by our clients require each giving opportunity to be tracked separately and they don't offer a straightforward way to track engagement opportunities let alone associate them with giving opportunities. If this is the case for your system, you'll need to separate out each component of the Cycle into separate records and develop clear protocols for how you capture a strategic interaction that covers more than one Cycle.

Capacity, Interest, Alignment, and Connection Ratings for a Prospect

Within the CRM system, you also want to capture your organization's internal Capacity, Interest, Alignment, and Connection ratings. These are values that are stored on the prospect's record. Rating systems vary across systems, but the general idea is to capture:

- **Capacity** - dollar ranges that indicate the donor's giving capacity (e.g., $500K–$999K, $1 million–$1.5 million, etc.), typically estimated over a 5-year period as well as for a single outright gift.
- **Interest** - the degree to which your research and learning about the prospect reveal they have interest in subjects that related to your organization's work (low/medium/high) or the number of interest areas (defined by your organization) that apply to the prospect.
- **Alignment** - a scale that represents how closely the donor's motivations and aspirations align to your organization's mission (e.g., 0 to 5 scale or minimal/moderate/strong rating).
- **Connection** - a value that indicates the degree to which the prospect is connected to your organization through personal engagement; and who they know (e.g., 1-4, where 1 indicates the donor is engaged in one way (e.g., volunteerism) and 3 indicates they have known relationships with 4 people connected to your organization (e.g., one board member, one staff member, one former staff member, and one transformational gift donor).

Note: in an ideal world, Interest and Connection ratings would be calculated by your CRM system.

Ask Readiness Rating for a Strategic Relationship Management Cycle

Another internal rating to track within the CRM system is an Ask Readiness rating. This value is stored on the Strategic Relationship

Management Cycle record and indicates how close you believe the prospect is to being ready to be asked for the gift and engagement opportunities that pertain to the cycle (e.g., now, within 1 month, 2-3 months, 6 months, 9 months, 1 year).

Other Data Elements

There are a couple dozen more data elements associated with a prospect (e.g., prospect type, prospect source, prospect status, cultivation team members), a Strategic Relationship Management Cycle (e.g., stewardship strategy), and strategic interactions (what the prospect will learn, what we will learn) that are necessary to track to enable you to monitor, analyze, and manage the transformational gift pipeline. Those data elements will be dependent on your specific implementation of *The Transformational Giving Playbook*™ project.

Automated Workflow

To cut back on the significant amount of time it takes organizations to manage acknowledgement and recognition processes by hand, you'll want to take advantage of automated workflow capabilities within your CRM. For example, when a transformational gift is posted, the CRM should automatically create an acknowledgement task for each appropriate staff member in accordance with your protocols. Similarly, when a gift is posted, the donor should be automatically added to the appropriate recognition lists (e.g., FY## annual report listing).

CRM Reports to Create

Potential Prospect Status Report

Having an organization-wide report that provides visibility into the current status of all **potential** prospects—those within the Identification and Qualification stages—ensures that no prospects "fall through the cracks" by not being assigned a Relationship Manager to shepherd them through the rest of the Strategic Relationship Management Cycle. See the Appendix for an example.

Missing Opportunities Report

Development Leadership should be able to confirm that all "Qualified" or "Assigned" prospects (i.e., the current pipeline) have at least one SRMC record in your CRM system with a stage of Qualification, Strategy, Cultivation, or Solicitation. This will help Leadership determine if there are any constituents not being tended to who should be.

Relationship Manager Portfolio Tracking Report

Relationship Managers should be able to quickly determine how they are progressing against their fundraising goals, where each of their prospects are in their current Strategic Relationship Management Cycle, and what the portfolio is forecasted to bring in. See the Appendix for a mock-up.

Strategic Interaction Tracking Report

Strategic interactions are key to successful cultivation. It's important that Cultivation Teams plan these for each transformational gift prospect in a Strategic Relationship Management Cycle, and that they take place at a frequency that is meaningful for the prospect and serves to advance the relationship. This report will help you monitor what's happened and what's coming up for transformational gift prospects. See the Appendix for a mock-up of this report.

Fundraising Progress Report

Relationship Managers, supervisors and senior leaders should be able to view a high-level report showing how much money has been raised toward the overall revenue goal for a given fiscal year, at any time. Fundraising progress should be reportable at a Relationship Manager, department, office, or organizational level.

All CRM systems can typically report on progress to varying degrees, but many do not track goals. Consequently, to prepare a Fundraising Progress Report may require you to use a different reporting tool alongside your CRM and to track goals outside the CRM. See the Appendix for a mock-up.

Note: This report should be made available for each Transformational Gifts Pipeline Meeting.

Revenue Forecast Report

Each fundraiser, department, and office, and the organization writ large, should be able to generate a report that forecasts revenue for the year. At the simplest level this involves being able to associate a default percent probability with each stage of the Strategic Relationship Management Cycle then multiplying that probability factor by the Expected Amount for each active opportunity. A more complex but useful approach is to develop an algorithm that takes into account a donor's Capacity, Interest, Alignment, and Connection ratings and the Ask Readiness rating for the Cycle. See the Appendix for a mock-up of this report.

Note: This report should be made available for each Transformational Gifts Pipeline Meeting.

Pipeline Meeting Report (used to prepare for pipeline meetings)

Moderators of pipeline meetings should be able to view all the opportunities in Strategy, Cultivation, and/or Solicitation (with Cultivation being the most important stage), with the ability to filter and sort the data in any way that is helpful, to determine which prospects should be discussed at each pipeline meeting. Regardless of whether your organization is federated, you should hold one cross-regional pipeline meeting for transformational gift prospects vs. one pipeline meeting per office.

Note: This report should be made available for each Transformational Gifts Pipeline Meeting.

Solicitor Credit Report

To recognize and reward a Relationship Manager for the gifts secured from their portfolio, you want to generate Solicitor Credit Reports. Solicitor credit is a complicated and often controversial topic within nonprofits.

It is complicated because a) there are multiple options for how solicitor credit can be awarded, and b) there are instances when more than one person might be a candidate for receiving solicitor credit but an organization is limited (by its CRM system or otherwise) in how credit can be shared.

It is controversial because limitations on how solicitation credit can be awarded or shared encourage staff to hoard donors and "jockey" for solicitor credit. This is typically based on the perceived degree of effort they put into cultivating a donor compared to someone else.

Robert Bull, a twenty year+ fundraising expert, once described to me three basic options nonprofits use to award solicitor credit:

1. **Relationship Manager-Based Credit**, where 100% of the gift is credited to the Relationship Manager.
2. **Fixed-Split Shared Credit**, where a percentage of the gift is awarded to the Relationship Manager and the remaining percentage is awarded to the fundraising staff person who secondarily provided the most assistance or support. The split is fixed in this option (e.g., 70/30, 80/20) and applies organization wide.
3. **Case-by-Case Shared Credit**, where a percentage of the gift is awarded to each fundraising staff person involved in the cultivation of the donor for that particular Strategic Relationship Management Cycle. The percentage splits are based on an analysis of each fundraising staff person's contributions to the cultivation process.

Of course, there can be all sorts of flavors in between.

Of these three basic options, we recommend nonprofits adopt a Relationship Manager-based approach to awarding solicitor credit. Awarding full credit to the Relationship Manager simplifies things from a process and technology perspective and encourages Relationship Managers to remain acutely focused on ensuring top notch cultivation and stewardship for the prospects and donors within their portfolio. That said, for that method to work and be palatable to all staff, it means organizations need a way to recognize others for the role they play, and this is where the concept of assist credit comes in.

See the Appendix for a Solicitor Credit Report mock-up.

Assist Credit Report

To recognize and reward program and administrative staff—even volunteer leaders—for the role they play in fundraising, and to recognize fundraisers for the support they lend in closing gifts for donors outside their portfolio, we recommend creating an Assist Credit Report. The Assist Credit Report should be based on the number of strategic interactions a staff person carries out for specific prospect. Your organization should determine the number of interactions that should result in assist credit for a gift. Our recommendation is at least three. See the Appendix for a mock-up.

Cultivation Team and Strategy Report (for a single prospect)

Relationship Managers, Development leadership, and senior leadership should be able to generate a Cultivation Team & Strategy Report for any opportunity (and by implication, a specific prospect). This report should contain the following key sections to ensure the reader can get a sense of who the prospect is, who is part of the effort to cultivate them, and where your organization is going with the prospect: prospect overview, understanding of the prospect, giving and engagement opportunities to pursue, the Cultivation Team assigned to the prospect, the strategic cultivation interactions that have been planned for the prospect, and modifications to any organizational communications the prospect is receiving while they are under cultivation.

Note: This report should be made available for each Transformational Gifts Pipeline Meeting in which the prospect will be discussed.

Stewardship Plan Report (for a single prospect)

Relationship Managers, Development leadership, and senior leadership should be able to generate a Stewardship Plan Report for a specific opportunity (and by implication, a specific prospect). This report should contain the strategy to be used to steward the gift and the strategic stewardship interactions that have been planned for the donor.

Templates to Track What Your CRM System May Not

To make it easy to track information that may not be easily captured and reported in your CRM system, we have created a number of templates you can download from our website at:

transformationalgivingplaybook.com/TGPtemplates

These include a:

- **Cultivation Team Template** to capture the Relationship Manager, Relationship Strategists, Natural Partners, and Program Partners. You can modify the template to track additional roles that are needed for your organization.
- **Cultivation Strategy Template** to capture an Overview of the Prospect, your Understanding of the Prospect, Giving and Engagement Opportunities to Pursue and Planned Strategic Cultivation Interactions for a Strategic Relationship Management Cycle, and modifications to Organizational Communications the prospect is receiving while they are a transformational gift prospect.
- **Corporate Fundraising Partner Meeting Template** to capture your meeting objectives, agenda, and meeting notes.
- **Acknowledgement & Recognition Protocol Template** to track, by giving level, the specific acknowledgements and recognition a donor should receive, from whom, and when.
- **Stewardship Plan Template** to capture the stewardship strategy for the Strategic Relationship Management Cycle and the planned strategic stewardship interactions you expect to have with a donor for the lifetime of their gift.
- **Transformational Goal Setting Template** to help you outline the six components of Transformational Goal Setting—the Focus Area, Theme, Good/Better/Best goals, Key Strategy, Outcome Influencers, and Tasks. You can use this template to configure your CRM system to track fundraiser, department, office, and organizational progress.

Emerging Trends and Technologies

Written with the Partners of Barker & Scott Consulting

CRM solutions are what a nonprofit primarily relies on to support its fundraising efforts, and it is worth noting that we expect more and more nonprofits to take advantage of emerging trends and newer technologies to inform and enhance those efforts, including high-touch fundraising.

Here are a few insights on what we are seeing.

Data Privacy and Security

Any technology that captures or processes data on individuals will have an impact on privacy and data security. When considering emerging or innovative technologies, a privacy impact assessment is important to understanding and complying with social norms and relevant regulations. Transparency about data collection, utilization, and sharing practices is paramount for engendering and maintaining trust, so organizations should engage constituents in defining the boundaries wherever possible. All staff should be very conscious of information security issues and implement proper security controls, with an institutional approach to risk management.

Artificial Intelligence (AI) and Machine Learning

The ability of machines to learn from data and take or inform actions and decisions will be a driving force of CRM. Fundraisers will start to leverage AI-driven insights and alerts more to determine how their time, on any given day, might be put to the highest and best use. AI can tell you who you haven't reached out to in a while. Who you should contact to take a specific action based on seasonality or cyclical factors. Who did something out of the ordinary. Who isn't on your radar that should be. AI can even learn how different people interact with a constituent and the language they use to craft communications based on that learning, so fundraisers don't have to think of it on their own or write communications from scratch.

Business Intelligence and Big Data

Business Intelligence is becoming increasingly democratized within organizations, with more advanced capabilities available to a broader set of roles. These capabilities offer more timely access to useful information, presented in a usable format that is tailored to the context of the individual user and the particular setting or task they are working on. For example, geo-location and/or facial recognition data can be combined with CRM data to automatically present a fundraiser with key highlights of a donor they may be about to meet with, along with program delivery data that matches that donor's personal interests, right on their smartphone (or any other device they may be using).

To identify good prospects, we expect nonprofits to move beyond traditional wealth and capacity overlays to leveraging behavioral and other data inside the organization, including advocacy, attendance, volunteerism, in-kind giving; and outside the organization, including websites donors visit, and segmentation donors fall into within companies that track their behavior across the internet. Nonprofits should leverage that data with data-mining algorithms to build predictive models. These models identify major and transformational gift prospects, donors with additional propensity to give and those at risk of churn, and "like" candidates. The models additionally inform Artificial Intelligence and personalization engines across digital and online channels, among other uses. Once nonprofit organizations have implemented stable CRM systems and related solutions such as digital experience and analytics platforms, they will be able to leverage the data they collect and use it to inform needed decisions

Internet of Things (IoT)

High-touch fundraisers are becoming increasingly reliant on "connected" smart phones and tablets that regularly collect and transmit data and technologies, which can transform personal experiences. This technology is being used for everything from personalizing content on digital signage and donor recognition displays or museum exhibits, to providing customized wayfinding, such as guiding people directly to their table at a Gala, or to the nearest open parking space or restroom. Data captured can include time spent at a particular location such as an exhibit or VIP lounge and can be fed into CRM systems for use in AI-enabled predictive modeling, or real-time alerting. IoT is being used in conservation and disaster relief settings to capture detailed data and situational intelligence about conditions and the impact of interventions, and this data is then used by Measurement and Evaluation (M&E) tools to craft compelling, evidence-based impact stories that appeal to funders and generate support.

Natural Language Processing

The technology for democratizing access to data is here, and nonprofits are embracing it in increasing numbers. With natural language processing, end-users will rely less and less on technical querying to ask questions about data, and they will more easily capture data into systems. For example, without knowing anything about technical querying, a Relationship Manager can type questions they want answered in the natural language of data: What was John Smith's last gift? What is the status of my portfolio by stage? And users can speak into their smartphone, PC, or smart speaker to add an interaction or a note to a donor's record.

Facial Recognition

In certain segments of the nonprofit sector, use of facial recognition will become more prominent in transformational gift fundraising. Museums and art centers, for example, are using this technology to send greeters to meet top donors and VIPs shortly after they arrive on-site, or to provide check-in free VIP lounge access. Nonprofits are using facial recognition to track attendance at events such as free performances, lectures, rallies and workshops, where it might otherwise be difficult to capture attendee data. This technology can also be used to identify each individual attendee rather than just the individual who registered for an event. Engagement data such as visits and time spent at exhibits can all be fed into the prospect research used to create a more fulfilling cultivation or stewardship experience.

Robotic Process Automation (RPA)

Don't let the name fool you, RPA has nothing to do with robotics. It's all about automating workflows such as data entry and other repeatable tasks. While this has greater utilization in low-touch fundraising, it can be relevant for transformational gift fundraising to automate manual workflows such as tax receipt processing, pledge management, grant reporting, endowment management and general document management.

Extended Reality (Augmented Reality, Virtual Reality)

As donor interactions and cultivation events move increasingly online, extended reality technologies including augmented reality (think Pokémon GO), virtual reality (a headset that allow you to tour a site virtually), and mixed reality (such as Microsoft's HoloLens) will present opportunities for donors to engage with your organization and mission in new, different, and more convenient ways. Prospects and Donors can visit a University or a Museum, interact with experts, leaders, and VIPs, or tour a conservation site in an immersive way without leaving their living room. This can provide a truly engaging, transformative, up-close experience and insider access that would not be possible or as scalable otherwise.

Gift

It is the transformational gift, or a number of them, that ultimately enables an organization to transform its impact. And this is what *The Transformational Giving Playbook*™ is all about—enabling nonprofits to raise more money, so you can do more good. But often overlooked, is how the giving of a transformational gift transforms the giver as well—especially when fundraisers understand and align to what matters most to the prospect. For an individual, corporation, or foundation to give at capacity, their gift needs to be aligned in three important ways:

Aligned To The Giver's Motivations

As individuals, our motivations are what get us out of bed every day. Our motivations are what give us meaning, purpose and a feeling of fulfillment. Every human has intrinsic motivations, whether we are able to articulate them or not. At a primal level, each of us is motivated to either survive or thrive, and as we move through our day, one of the things we're all looking for, even on an unconscious level, is this: Will this thing (car, person, food, organization, or donation) help me survive or thrive?

When we have a more conscious awareness of what our motivations are—what gives us meaning or a sense of purpose—we are better able to consciously determine whether or not something helps fulfill that.

The point here is to understand that each of your prospects and donors—whether you are speaking with them as individuals or as employees of a corporation or foundation—is guided, consciously or unconsciously, by their intrinsic motivations. They are seeking ways to give their life a deeper sense of meaning, purpose, and fulfillment. And they will only give at capacity if they feel that the giving of the gift gives them that deeper sense of meaning, purpose and fulfillment.

This is underscored by the *2021 Bank of America Study of Philanthropy: Charitable Giving by Affluent Households*, conducted in partnership with the Indiana University Lilly Family School of Philanthropy. When 1,626 high net worth households were asked how they determine which nonprofit organizations to support, 71.5% indicated that they draw upon their personal values to make that decision. Interest in the issue addressed by the organization was second to this, at 57.2%.

Corporations are no different. Although in the past a company's purpose may have been something held more personally by the company founder or CEO, more and more companies are realizing the value of having clear company values that include social responsibility.

Likewise, in evaluating their nonprofit grantees, foundations look for evidence of alignment of the nonprofit's work with the foundation's mission before awarding funding.

The job of the fundraiser is to learn what the prospect's intrinsic motivations are and—if indeed the mission of your nonprofit is aligned with the prospect's motivations—to demonstrate how their gift can help them fulfill that purpose.

So how do we discover a prospect's intrinsic motivations? Quite simply, we ask.

Each strategic interaction conducted as part of the Cultivation process represents an opportunity to dive deeper.

It bears repeating here some questions that will help you identify a prospect's motivations:

- What draws you (or your organization) to this work?
- How did you (or your organization's leadership) become passionate about this cause?
- What are the things that motivate you in your life, your work, your giving?

- Tell me, at the end of the day, what it is that gives your life meaning and purpose?
- Tell me, at the end of the day, what societal problems are you looking to solve?
- What would you say your WHY is—the thing that motivates you (or your employees) every day to do what you do?

Here are some examples of motivations.

- Dana is motivated by their love of nature that was instilled in them through family hiking, camping, and kayaking trips.
- Harshali is motivated by her love for dogs which played a huge part in helping her navigate childhood as a differently abled person.
- Steve is motivated by the death of his brother to drugs and doesn't want any other family to have to go through what his went through.

Granted, these types of conversations may be different than what you're used to, but they will have a profound effect on your ability to connect with a prospect, and it is an important starting place for determining if this prospect is aligned with the mission of the organization and, therefore, important to consider as a transformational gift prospect.

Aligned To The Giver's Aspirations

If motivations are about a sense of fulfillment, aspirations are about a sense of accomplishment. Our aspirations are about who we want to be, what we want to do, what we want to have, and the legacy we want to leave.

Our aspirations tap into the need each of us has for significance—to feel important and needed.

Individuals will only give at capacity if they feel that the gift will help fulfill their aspirations and provide that sense of significance.

Similarly, many corporations and foundations also seek to intentionally make a difference in the world and leave a legacy. For example, KIND, maker of healthy snacks, is about creating a kinder, more empathetic world by discovering our shared humanity and embracing the power of our differences. The Bill and Melinda Gates Foundation believes the path out of poverty begins when the next generation can access quality healthcare and a great education.

Once again, the job of the fundraiser is to ascertain what the aspirations of the donor are and if the mission of your organization can help to further and fulfill those aspirations, then demonstrate how it can do that.

Your strategic interactions are the perfect time to ask questions that help identify the donor's aspirations.

It bears repeating here some questions that will help you identify a donor's aspirations. They are written for an individual but can be tweaked for a corporation or foundation.

- 1 year, 5 years, 10 years from now, what are some of the goals you want to achieve?
- What's the legacy you want to leave?
- What do you most want to be remembered for?
- What's on your bucket list? What are the fun things you want to do before you die?
- What is it that you would love to accomplish in your life?
- What is it that you would love to accomplish in relation to this cause?

Here are some examples of aspirations that are related to the example motivations listed above:

- Dana wants to play a significant role in the protection and designation of national parks and conservation land throughout the U.S. but is particularly interested in the regions along the Appalachian Trail.

- Harshali aspires to create a vehicle through which differently abled children have free access to companion dogs. This includes working with reputable dog breeders, creating dog training centers based on Harshali's training method, an application process for families, and placement mentorship and training for the child.
- Steve aspires to be involved in the creation of comprehensive and innovative drug intervention programs that include everything from access to alternative treatments to family support retreat centers where families can support one another.

As with motivations, learning about a donor's aspirations will have a profound effect on your ability to connect with them, and it is an important starting place for determining if this prospect is aligned with the mission of the organization.

Case Study: Michael and Pam

Michael is a Senior Managing Director at a global investment firm. He and his wife Pam have always had a heart for those in need, always cared about the underdog, always been driven by empathy.

As a result, contributing to City Year was a natural fit for them. City Year is an organization that provides, through young City Year AmeriCorps members, direct success coaching to students within local schools so all students can thrive.

Michael and Pam first became interested in City Year in 2013 when their daughter, Jesse, volunteered at a school in Boston.

They loved the mission of City Year because it aligned with their values. They loved the impact they could make, so they started supporting the organization at the transformational gift level every year, for several years.

Then came the "seminal moment," as Michael describes it.

In 2014, their daughter was helping to run a summer training program. One of the speakers at the event was the Executive Director of an international affiliate of City Year in South Africa. Michael and his wife were planning to travel to South Africa two months later and made plans to visit the site there.

When they toured a City Year school in Johannesburg as part of their visit, Michael said, "That's when we saw the light."

South Africa is stunningly beautiful—the country, the culture, and the people. Equally stunning though, is the extreme poverty and high unemployment that exists against such a beautiful backdrop. Many students are unlikely to have an opportunity to go to college, so the City Year experience is seminal in their lives. There was an opportunity to strengthen City Year South Africa's operations in support of longer-term financial sustainability, so the organization could have greater impact for the students and young adults involved in the program. Michael and Pam could directly see how impactful their support could be.

So that year they started supporting City Year South Africa, as well as City Year operations in the U.S., and tripled their giving. They have since shifted all of their City Year support to the South Africa affiliate and continue to give at the transformational gift level.

But Michael and Pam recognize there's still more they can do.

Subsequently, in addition to City Year, Michael and Pam began to support several other organizations. They are very clear about the kinds of organizations they support—organizations that align with their values of equality, and organizations that help poor kids held back by the effects of systemic racism get "a leg up" by closing the education gap, and the health care gap. And they strive to work with smaller, relatively unknown organizations where their support and dollars can make a significant difference.

Michael and Pam have increased their giving to all the organizations they support.

Michael and Pam's motivation is simple: it's the right thing to do.

When we asked Michael what legacy he wants to leave, he reflected back to a funeral he attended in his 30s. The person giving the eulogy talked about the legacy the recently departed person had created, and in reflecting on those words, Michael wasn't yet sure what he wanted his legacy to be.

Today he knows what his legacy is.

"I want people to know that we tried to make a difference. That we tried to help those who start out with a disadvantage, due to reasons beyond their control, by giving them the opportunity they rightfully deserve to succeed."

~~~~

Aligned To The Organization's Mission

"I think a hero is any person really intent on making this a better place for all people."

~ Maya Angelou

When your organization can demonstrate how your mission, and the organizational apparatus to achieve that mission, provides a way for a donor to fulfill their intrinsic motivations and aspirations—far beyond what they could ever do on their own—it becomes a compelling reason for the donor to give a truly transformational gift. Because in doing so, it enables the donor to be the person they aspire to be, to fulfill their personal dream, and to become a champion to a cause they believe in.

This provides donors with a truly transformational experience, and it gives you the ability to attract the brightest and best philanthropists who can help your organization transform its impact.
~~~~

Let's Take a Look at Where We've Been …

In this book, we've shown how *The Transformational Giving Playbook*™ enables you to go FROM …

1. **A heavy reliance on the art of fundraising**, where fundraisers primarily rely on artful elements like intuition, charm, and a sense of timing … **TO elevating the art of fundraising by leveraging science** and proven strategies, along with innovative technology, research, tools, and clearly defined business processes.

2. **Looking to extrinsic motivators, like "the right" case materials** to convey the importance of the mission … TO **a focus on understanding and aligning to the intrinsic motivations and aspirations of the donor** and demonstrating how the mission and apparatus of the organization can help the donor fulfill both, in a way they never could on their own. Ultimately, this makes a far more compelling case for donors to give at capacity.

3. **Too much dependence on fundraising "superstars,"** which can leave an organization vulnerable when they leave … TO **positioning "superstars" as mentors** to their peers, sharing their best practices, and most importantly, sharing how they THINK.

4. **A lack of training and models for new, inexperienced fundraisers**, leaving them to figure things out on their own … TO **equipping fundraisers with the skill set they need to be successful**—through training, mentorship, step-by-step roadmaps, and skill-building.

5. **Spending too much time going after gifts that are too small to be transformational**, which means fundraisers won't generate the transformational gifts required to move the needle on the mission in a significant way … TO **prioritizing the time, energy and**

efforts of the Development department on donors who have the capacity to give truly transformational gifts.

6. **A lack of clearly defined business processes**, where everyone does things differently, which ultimately puts risks the organization and donor relationship at risk … TO **clear business processes**, standards, expectations, accountability, and coordination **designed for everyone to win**.

7. **A lack of the right tools for fundraisers to effectively perform their jobs**, resulting in a heavy reliance on Excel spreadsheets and Word documents, which makes fundraising less effective … TO **a comprehensive set of leading-edge tools** that provide consistency, transparency, and effectiveness in the fundraising efforts across the organization.

8. **A deeply ingrained "my donor" mindset**, causing fundraisers to "wall off" their donors, creating winners and losers within the organization … TO **creating a unified donor experience** that significantly grows revenue across the whole of the organization.

9. **A reluctance of program staff to support fundraising efforts**, because even though their input is vital, program staff often receive little or no recognition for the work they do to support fundraising … TO **creating a culture of philanthropy** where every staff person is recognized and rewarded for how they contribute to the financial health of the organization.

10. **Prioritizing recruitment of board members with domain expertise or name recognition** who are willing to give meaningful advice but not always willing to give or get meaningful gifts … TO **prioritizing recruitment of board members who are willing to make a significant financial commitment** and bring other transformational gift donors into the fold.

All of this is what enables you to go **from incremental, stagnant, or negative growth**, where your organization is struggling to raise money for your mission—thereby putting your organization, your staff, and the mission at risk—**to exponential growth**, where you are raising significantly more money through a focus on six and seven-figure transformational gifts, which ultimately provide the capacity to do WAY more good.

Next Steps

So, what do you do next? How do you take everything we've talked about in *The Transformational Giving Playbook*™, and begin transforming fundraising in your organization?

To be successful, there are three things you need.

First, you need to know WHAT to do.

That's what we've shared with you in this book. We've given you a detailed road map to follow so you can move from incremental, stagnant, or negative growth as an organization, where you are struggling to have the impact you want to have at the level you want to have it, to exponential growth, where you—like Facing History or City Year—completely transform your organization, your teams, your donors, and your impact, because you took an approach to fundraising that focused on:

- aligning the donor's motivations and aspirations with the mission of your organization,
- enabling all fundraisers to be winners by equipping them with the Strategic Relationship Management Cycle, the tools, and the skills they need to elevate the art and science of fundraising, and
- creating a larger context for transformation by starting at the top of your organization, with transformational leadership that calls everyone to be their best, shared guiding principles for fundraising that bring everyone together on the same page, and transformational goals that inspire staff, board members and donors alike.

You have the WHAT in your hands. But that's not all you need.

Second, you need to know HOW to do it.

How do you change your leadership style from transactional to transformational? How do you get all fundraisers to understand and embrace the science of fundraising? How do you craft your Transformational Story? How do you do the research to identify new transformational gift prospects? How do you conduct a Pipeline meeting? How do you make the Ask? And how do you configure your CRM to capture and report the information you need on transformational gift prospects? For this, whenever possible, we have provided examples, templates, checklists, blueprints, and guidelines. You can access these resources at:

transformationalgivingplaybook.com/TGPtemplates.

But there are always those things that can't be captured in a template, checklist, or blueprint. How do you handle a team member who's used to being the superstar fundraiser and is now being asked to mentor others? How do you work with your organization to create a concise set of Guiding Principles for Fundraising? What's the best way to retain your transformational gift donors year over year? These are the kinds of things that are learned "on the ground" and with the support of others who have gone before.

So, you have to know what to do and how to do it, but it is the third thing that separates those organizations that exponentially transform their impact through a transformational gifts program from those who don't.

Third, you need to TAKE ACTION.

In other words, you need to actually implement *The Transformational Giving Playbook*™. You need to prepare the organization for a new comprehensive approach to fundraising, and then take the action, train the board, equip the teams, configure the CRM, implement a Strategic Relationship Management Cycle, do the research, establish the Cultivation Teams, build the relationships, conduct the Transformational Gifts Pipeline Meetings, conduct Transformational Goal Setting to define your GBB goals, Outcome Influencers, and Tasks … and actually do it.

And that's the hard, but rewarding work, of implementing a Transformational Giving program.

If you know this is the next right step for your organization, and for your mission, then there are really just two ways to go about it.

Do It Yourself

The first way is to do it yourself. To take everything we've given you here in *The Transformational Giving Playbook*™ framework—together with the templates, the guidelines, the examples, the checklists, and the blueprints—put a team together, starting at the top, share your vision for what's possible for your mission and your organization, and create an implementation plan.

We recommend the project be sponsored by the Chief Development Officer. A Steering Committee should be established that includes the CDO, CEO, CFO, and possibly the board's Development Committee Chair. Additionally, a Core Project Team of representative staff from each high-touch fundraising program—across headquarters and the chapters/sites/regional offices—should be assembled to customize *The Transformational Giving Playbook*™ to your organization. You'll also want to have a Project Manager/Coordinator to arrange for the active participation of staff and consolidate feedback on each component of your Playbook.

Our experience is that a typical *Transformational Giving Playbook*™ project takes nine to twelve months. Organizational culture, team dynamics, resource availability, the state of your CRM system, fundraiser experience, and time needed by staff to absorb the change, are all factors that impact the timing.

Get Some Help

Of course, the second way to implement *The Transformational Giving Playbook*™ is to get some help. And that's what the TGP Consulting team specializes in. We've been up this "Everest" before, and we view it as both our privilege and responsibility to get you up the mountain as quickly, safely, and successfully as we can.

How TGP Consulting Can Help You

Our Reason for Being

We believe nonprofits are uniquely positioned to solve the world's most challenging problems.

Nonprofits are in the business of making the world a better place, and so are we.

- We believe this planet is sacred and it is our responsibility to care for and protect it.
- We believe in equal justice and opportunity for all.
- We believe in science and its capacity to bring clarity to our understanding of ourselves and the world.
- We believe in the arts and its imaginative power to liberate the human spirit.
- We believe access to knowledge provides the means for every human being to realize their greatest potential.

TGP Consulting exists for one reason and one reason only: to help nonprofits raise more money to do more good.

The problem is most fundraising strategies are just too slow and ineffective to meet the urgency of the moment.

The solution, we believe, is to focus on transformational gifts in order to exponentially increase your revenue quickly.

We bring the experience and expertise to help you build both the institutional and individual infrastructure required to achieve your big, bold fundraising goals. Or as we like to say, we give you the best, most innovative high performance "race car" and then coach, mentor, and train your team to believe, think, and act like championship "race car drivers."

How We Work

Should you choose to work with us, this is what you can expect.

Our Team

Your project will be staffed by seasoned professionals, each of whom has a decade (or more!) of experience in nonprofit fundraising. Our unique backgrounds, experience, and expertise enable us to support every aspect of your transformational gift fundraising. Moreover, all of our team members are creative, analytical, inspirational, emotionally intelligent, and deeply committed to serving nonprofits.

Our Process

A few important things to know about our process:

- We help you maximize your philanthropy **from day one**.
- We hold nothing back; we **transfer our intellectual property to you**.
- **We build capacity within you** as individuals and as an organization so you can be self-sufficient.
- ...That said, we'd be honored to continue to **partner with you as long as you want**, as thought partners, mentors, coaches, and advisors.

More specifically, we work with you on two tracks simultaneously. 1) We work with you on developing the **institutional infrastructure**—through comprehensive processes, systems, and tools—to support a successful transformational giving program, and 2) we work with you on developing the **individual infrastructure**—through coaching, mentorship, and skills training—to equip your team members with the competence and confidence to fundraise at a transformational gift level.

On the institutional side, we'll initiate a comprehensive process to better understand your organization and your unique challenges, mission, culture, and goals. We want to understand where you are, and then help you envision what you can become. From there, we will leave no stone unturned as we work with you to define everything from:

- Your Guiding Principles for Fundraising,
- Your detailed business processes across the entire Strategic Relationship Management Cycle,
- Your framework for transformational gift pipeline meetings,
- The new fields, reports, and workflow you need to configure in your CRM system.

Out of this in-depth project, your organization will have the foundation for a proven transformational giving program.

The final step will be the rollout of the transformational giving program to the larger organization, which you can either take on yourselves, or we can work with you to ensure the successful implementation of The Playbook.

Although it's impossible to guarantee results, what we can say is that every organization who has wholeheartedly implemented the strategies in *The Transformational Giving Playbook*™, has exponentially increased their revenue (as you read in the case studies we've included), which has significantly increased their ability to successfully carry out their mission.

Other Benefits

In addition to all of this, our clients have also noticed some important unexpected benefits:

Greater competence level among the staff by receiving specific training to help them develop their fundraising skills.

Greater confidence. With increased competence comes increased confidence. And with increased confidence comes greater joy and job satisfaction.

Greater community. *The Transformational Giving Playbook™* is intentionally designed so that everyone wins, which ultimately reduces competition between departments, offices/chapters, and staff.

How To Connect With Us

It would be a privilege to guide your organization through this process. If that sounds like the next right step for your organization, I encourage you to reach out to me directly at lisa@tgp-consulting.com to explore the possibilities.

Postface

By Lisa Scott

This book first published during the Coronavirus pandemic, concurrent with worldwide protests in support of racial justice. I am acutely aware of the challenges that nonprofits are facing during this challenging time, so it was important to me that I get this first edition in your hands as soon as possible. My sincere hope is that *The Transformational Giving Playbook*™ offers you new, innovative and comprehensive guidance that helps you raise exponentially more money, so your organization can not only survive the pandemic but thrive in the years and decades to come.

But there is more to be said. Beyond the need to significantly increase revenue, for which this book provides guidance, there are two other significant challenges facing the nonprofit sector that this book does not speak to:

1. Racism in philanthropy.
2. The risks that wealth inequality poses for the nonprofit sector.

Racism in Philanthropy

Philanthropy in the U.S. is white-dominant. When I think of the many hundreds of fundraisers I have engaged with over the last 20+ years, I can count on two hands the number of Development staff who are people of color. And whenever I've asked Gift Officers what percentage of their high-net-worth prospects and donors are people of color, the answer has always been none or very few.

There is considerable work for nonprofits to do to create the conditions that attract high-net-worth people of color into their donor ranks.

Why is this important? Because donors of color care very much about their communities. They care about education, social justice, gender equity, racial justice, and the environment, among many other concerns. And, they have unique and valuable perspectives on how to lead, how to innovate, how to prioritize and invest, and how to create positive, lasting change that nonprofits are missing, and from which they cannot reap the benefits.

One of the ways a nonprofit can begin to address racial injustice in philanthropy and recruit more donors of color to contribute to your mission in meaningful ways is by delivering a Curated Connection Experience that speaks to them. We lay out the importance of the Curated Connection Experience in the Groundwork / Transformational System / Cultivation section of *The Transformational Giving Playbook™*. There is much more to be said about that experience for donors of color—but I'll leave that for another book.

For now, I will offer that it would be a mistake to assume that if your organization's senior leadership, staff, board, and transformational gift donors are predominantly white, that how you approach fundraising will appeal to and attract donors of color. Poverty/slum/ghetto tourism and a white savior complex are extremely problematic for donors of color. And these are just two examples of how racism rears its head in nonprofits.

The truth is, it takes diversity to relate to diversity, and it takes diversity to create a safe space that welcomes everyone into the fold. But an organization cannot become diverse until those who lead it are willing to share power. That is part of what it means to dismantle systemic racism, and the nonprofit sector, like the government and commercial sectors, has a lot of work to do.

The Risks of Wealth Inequality to the Nonprofit Sector

Since 2016, Inequality.org has published a Gilded Giving report. The organization's most recent report, *Gilded Giving 2022: How Wealth Inequality Distorts Philanthropy and Imperils Democracy* continues its look into how giving by the ultra-wealthy poses risks to the nonprofit sector independence, the integrity of the tax system, and the health of our democracy. In this recent report, the extent to which the charitable sector has been captured by the ultra-wealthy—exacerbated, in part by the pandemic—is laid out in stark terms.

Key takeaways from this and earlier reports for me are:

1. **The number of households making charitable donations continues to decline, while the amount of money being contributed by smaller and smaller numbers of billionaires and foundations is increasing.** To be specific, fewer than half of all U.S. households now give to charity, whereas top-heavy philanthropy has increased, with households making over $1 million accounting for 40% of charitable deductions in 2019. In addition, the size of what Giving USA defines as a mega-gift has grown from $30 million in 2011 to $450 million in 2021. This is worrisome because it a) makes funding unpredictable and b) puts the ultra-wealthy in a position to potentially 'set the terms' by which nonprofits operate, thereby compromising the autonomy and sustainability of the nonprofit sector and the scope of work nonprofits do in the world.

2. **The ultra-wealthy continue to capitalize on the tax advantages afforded them by the 2017 tax reform bill that took effect in 2018.** In fact, "the top two charitable causes of ultra-wealthy donors are their own private foundations and donor-advised funds" (DAFs), with gifts to these entities amounting to nearly one third of charitable giving in the U.S.

3. **Private foundations and DAFs aren't necessarily quick to distribute significant portions of that revenue to the charities they are designed to fund**, thereby hoarding funds that can be used to further enrich the ultra-wealthy.

4. **Impact investing and dynasty trusts are yet other tax-advantaged vehicles that can be used to divert funds from charities**, as a significant portion of impact investments are made through vehicles such as DAFs, and assets held in trust are not subject to taxation.

You might think there is a contradiction between the purpose of this book and the perils of wealth inequality as noted above. There isn't, but only if nonprofits are mindful of the influence of wealth on their organizations and missions and take measures to keep that influence "in check," and we as a citizenry work to achieve the report's recommended reforms to DAFs, private foundations, broad-based giving, and top-heavy philanthropy.

The ultra-wealthy have tremendous power in this country within the government and commercial sectors, and we cannot afford for the nonprofit sector to be held hostage or controlled by the powerful few. Yet, here's why transformational gifts are still important: **our planet as a whole and civic life and democracy in the U.S. would not survive for long without the work of nonprofits**. As I said in the introduction, nonprofits are the most willing, committed, and intentional about solving the world's greatest and most intractable problems. But for nonprofits to survive, thrive, and do their essential work, they need money.

The discussion in this book around aligning the donor's motivations and aspirations *with your organization's mission* is what's important. I have witnessed many nonprofits fall into the trap of accepting transformational gifts to fund a donor's 'pet project' or special interests instead of being on target with the mission. Nonprofits need to be very clear about their mission and refuse the temptation to shift it because of the intoxication of money and need to appease the ultra-wealthy.

To be continued...

Appendix

Indicators of Capacity, Interest, Alignment, and Connection

Individuals

Capacity

[ ] Provided an indicator of wealth such as job title or residence in a high-net-worth area
[ ] Made significant gifts to nonprofits in the past
[ ] Has a family foundation
[ ] Has prominent buildings, physical spaces, or programs named after them
[ ] Has a history of nonprofit board volunteerism or philanthropy
[ ] Is "new to money" and looking for an entrée into philanthropy (which means their donation history might be minimal and give a false sense that they are not philanthropically inclined)

Interest

[ ] Has an interest in subjects related to your organization's work
[ ] Donated to other nonprofits with a similar mission

Alignment

[ ] Has a connection to your mission or programmatic work
[ ] Expressed philanthropic aspirations to make a difference in a way that is aligned to your organization's mission

Connection

[ ] Is already engaged with your organization in some capacity (e.g., a volunteer)
[ ] Has a personal connection to a staff member, board member, or other transformational gift donor

Corporations

Capacity

[ ] Has annual revenues of comparable to other corporate transformational gift donors
[ ] Has an established giving program
[ ] Entered into partnership agreements with nonprofit organizations in the past
[ ] Sponsored large events on behalf of nonprofit organizations

Interest

[ ] Has brand alignment with your organization or is interested in brand exposure
[ ] Has marketing alignment with your organization
[ ] Has a social responsibility focus on areas related to your organization's work
[ ] Has a philanthropic interest in subjects related to your organization's work
[ ] Donated to other nonprofits with a similar mission

Alignment

[ ] Donated to or partnered with other organizations with a similar mission
[ ] Expressed social responsibility business objectives that are aligned to your organization's mission

Connection

[ ] Has leadership with a personal connection to your mission or programmatic work.
[ ] Has a connection to a staff member, board member, donor, or other transformational gift donor

Foundations

Capacity

[ ] Has assets of $10M+ or recent past giving of $100K outright
[ ] Made significant grants to nonprofits in the past

Interest

[ ] Has a philanthropic interest in subjects related to your organization's work
[ ] Has giving guidelines that fit squarely with your organization
[ ] Donated to other nonprofits with a similar mission

Alignment

[ ] Has a philanthropic mission and current focus area or funding program that is aligned to your organization's programmatic mission

Connection

[ ] Has a connection to a staff member, board member, donor, or other transformational gift donor

Cultivation Team Structure Examples

Here is a baseline Cultivation Team structure that can work for most nonprofits.

Depending upon how complex your organization is, you may need to define more roles. Next is a more complicated structure established by one of our clients.

Cultivation Team

COMPLEX STRUCTURE

Only the Relationship Director role is required. All other roles are optional, though it is anticpated Natural Partners and Program Partners will be added as the Cultivation Strategy for the prospect evolves.

(if appropriate)
One or More Staff
Serve as a coach or consultant to the Relationship Director in developing the strategy to secure a significant commitment and/or meet a strategic goal.

(when/if needed)
One or More Staff
An Escalation team is established only when needed. This team becomes the final arbiter of Cultivation Strategy when conflicts exist that cannot be resolved by the Relationship Director.

RELATIONSHIP DIRECTOR

(required)
One Staff

ASSISTANT RELATIONSHIP DIRECTOR

(if needed)
One Staff

Has overall accountability for the relationship, is the decision-maker for how to strategically advance the relationship (Relationship Director) and oversees the day-to-day execution of the Cultivation Strategy (Assistant Relationship Director). These roles should be fulfilled by a fundraiser.

LOCAL RELATIONSHIP PARTNERS

One or More Staff
Have responsibility for strategically advancing the relationship at a local level and carrying out key activities within the Cultivation Strategy, under the direction of the Relationship Director.

SUPPORT TEAM MEMBERS

One or More Staff
Provide support to the Relationship Director and other members of the Cultivation Team in a wide variety of ways (e.g., administrative support, messaging and communications, proposal writing, celebrity engagement, etc.).

NATURAL PARTNERS

(likely needed)
Many
Has an influential relationship (directly or indirectly) with a prospect that can be leveraged. The relationship may be pre-existing or develop during Cultivation.

PROGRAM PARTNERS

(likely needed)
One or More Staff
Serves as the "content team" by providing programmatic subject matter expertise to assist with the case for support. Post-commitment, Program Partners play a critical role in stewarding the donor's gift by communicating impact.

Transformational Gifts Pipeline Meeting Participation Model for a Federated Organization

This example participation model assumes a national organizational structure with chapter offices and no regional offices:

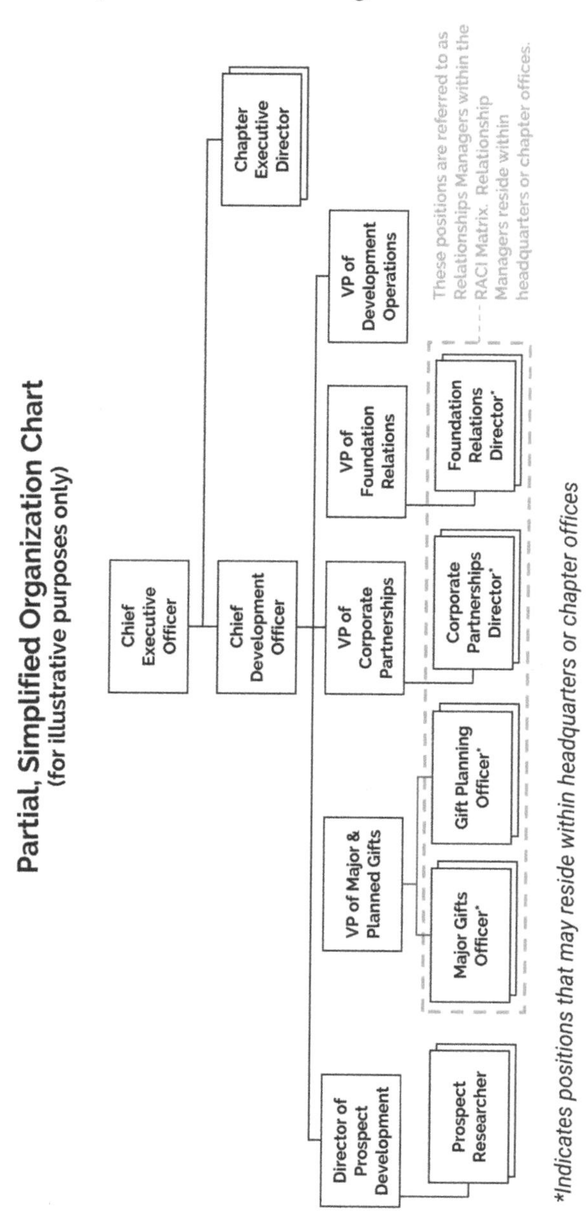

With this structure, you would hold Transformational Gifts Pipeline Meetings for each chapter as well as a meeting for headquarters, and the meeting participation plan would look like this:

Participation in Chapter Transformational Gifts Pipeline Meetings

Participants	Role	Responsibilities
VP of Major & Planned Gifts, VP of Corporate Partnerships, VP of Foundation Relations, and Chapter Executive Director	Strategic Advisors	Provides strategic guidance to Relationship Managers on Cultivation Strategy and solicitation approach, and ensures alignment of those strategies and approaches with the mission and organizational funding opportunities
Prospect Researcher assigned to support the chapter	Moderator	Determines what prospects will be discussed and sets the agenda for the meeting in consultation with the VPs, moderates the meeting to keep all participants on track with the agenda
Prospect Researcher assigned to support the chapter	Organizer	Schedules the pipeline meetings and disseminates the agenda and reports beforehand
Relationship Managers (i.e., Gift Officers and Directors) for the prospects being discussed	Facilitators	Facilitate the meeting discussion about each of their prospects and records changes to the Cultivation Team, Cultivation Strategy, and solicitation approach in the CRM
Program Partners and Other Staff (as needed, based on the prospects being discussed)	Contributors	Offer insights that further inform the alignment of programmatic work to the donor's motivations and aspirations, in addition to the Cultivation Strategy or solicitation approach

Participation in Headquarters Transformational Gifts Pipeline Meetings

Participants	Role	Responsibilities
Chief Development Officer (always) and the Chief Executive Officer (as needed, based on the prospects being discussed)	Strategic Advisors	Provides strategic guidance to Relationship Managers on Cultivation Strategy and solicitation approach, and ensures alignment of those strategies and approaches with the mission and organizational funding opportunities
Director of Prospect Development	Moderator	Determines what prospects will be discussed and sets the agenda for the meeting in consultation with the Chief Development Officer and Relationship Managers, moderates the meeting to keep all participants on track with the agenda
Director of Prospect Development or a Prospect Researcher	Organizer	Schedules the pipeline meetings and disseminates the agenda and reports beforehand
Relationship Managers (i.e., Gift Officers and Directors)	Facilitators	Facilitate the meeting discussion about each of their prospects and records changes to the Cultivation Team, Cultivation Strategy, and solicitation approach in the CRM
Program Partners and Other Staff (as needed, based on the prospects being discussed)	Contributors	Offer insights that further inform the alignment of programmatic work to the donor's motivations and aspirations, in addition to the Cultivation Strategy or solicitation approach
Major Gifts Officers, Corporate Partnerships Directors, Foundation Relations Directors, and Chapter Executive Directors and Development staff (as desired)	Observers	Listen to the discussion

We encourage other Chapter Development staff and Executive Directors to attend headquarters' Transformational Gifts Pipeline Meetings as desired. This level of transparency cuts back on concerns among chapters about being in competition with headquarters for revenue, even if organizational structures, revenue sharing, or chapter funding models foster competition.

Prospect Status Report Example

Constituent Name	Prospect Status	Prospect Status Date	Source of Prospect	Estimated Giving Capacity (over 5 Years)	External Giving Capacity	Relationship Manager
California						
Sandra Moran	Qualified	2/10	Self-identification	$250,000	Principal	
The Bird Company	Qualified	2/26	Referral	$100,000	Principal	
The Oster Family Foundation	Qualified	2/11	Cursory Research	$300,000	Principal	
Headquarters						
Floyd Cooper	Potential	2/13	Referral	$250,000	Principal	
Karen Green	Potential	1/18	Referral	$250,000	Transformational	
The Knox Foundation	Qualified	2/21	Online Research	$1,000,000	Transformational	
Jeremy Smith	Qualified	1/31	Wealth Screening	$1,500,000	Transformational	
Sandrine Spivy	Qualified	1/15	Self-identification	$1,000,000	Transformational	
Maryland						
Best City Foundation	Potential	2/15	Wealth Screening	$500,000	Principal	
Emilano Russo	Potential	1/12	Event Attendee	$100,000	Principal	
Leticia Smith	Qualified	2/11	Corporate Volunteer	$250,000	Principal	
Solar Enterprises	Qualified	2/17	Self-identification	$2,500,000	Transformational	
Solutions4Good	Qualified	2/10	Past Prospect	$500,000	Principal	

Relationship Manager Portfolio Tracking Report Mock-Up

Relationship Manager
Role

Fundraising Summary

Annual Fundraising Goal	$
Funds Raised to Date	$
Portfolio Capacity	$
Portfolio Size (# donors)	#
Average Strategic Interactions (1)	#
Most Recent Gift Closed Date	MM/DD/YY
Most Recent Gift Closed Amount	$

1) Average # for the prospects and donors within the portfolio

Strategic Relationship Management Cycle Overview

Stage	Number of Donors	Target Giving Amount	Forecasted Revenue (2)
Identification	#	$	$
Qualification	#	$	$
Strategy	#	$	$
Cultivation	#	$	$
Solicitation	#	$	$
Gift Processing, Acknowledgement & Recognition	#	$	$
Stewardship	#	$	$
Total	#	$	$

(2) Sum of (Probability x Target Gift Amount) for each cycle in this specified stage

Portfolio Overview

Name	Cycle	Stage	Target Giving Amount	Probability	Last Strategic Interaction	Last Strategic Interaction	Next Strategic Interaction Date	Next Strategic Interaction
ABC	ABC	ABC	$	%	MM/DD/YY		MM/DD/YY	
ABC	ABC	ABC	$	%	MM/DD/YY		MM/DD/YY	
ABC	ABC	ABC	$	%	MM/DD/YY		MM/DD/YY	
ABC	ABC	ABC	$	%	MM/DD/YY		MM/DD/YY	
ABC	ABC	ABC	$	%	MM/DD/YY		MM/DD/YY	
ABC	ABC	ABC	$	%	MM/DD/YY		MM/DD/YY	

Fundraising Progress Report Mock-Up

Office	Department	Staff	Revenue Raised to Date	Good Annual Fundraising Goal	Percentage of Good Goal Achieved	Better Annual Fundraising Goal	Percentage of Better Goal Achieved	Best Annual Fundraising Goal	Percentage of Best Goal Achieved
Organization			$ 18,000,000	$ 24,000,000	75%	$ 26,400,000	68%	$ 28,800,000	63%
California			$ 6,000,000	$8,000,000	75%	$8,800,000	68%	$9,600,000	63%
	Corporate Partnerhips		$ 1,500,000	$ 2,000,000	75%	$ 2,200,000	68%	$ 2,400,000	63%
		ABC	$ 750,000	$ 1,000,000	75%	$ 1,100,000	68%	$ 1,200,000	63%
		ABC	$ 750,000	$ 1,000,000	75%	$ 1,100,000	68%	$ 1,200,000	63%
	Foundation Relations		$ 1,500,000	$ 2,000,000	75%	$ 2,200,000	68%	$ 2,400,000	63%
		ABC	$ 750,000	$ 1,000,000	75%	$ 1,100,000	68%	$ 1,200,000	63%
		ABC	$ 750,000	$ 1,000,000	75%	$ 1,100,000	68%	$ 1,200,000	63%
	Major Gifts		$ 1,500,000	$ 2,000,000	75%	$ 2,200,000	68%	$ 2,400,000	63%
		ABC	$ 750,000	$ 1,000,000	75%	$ 1,100,000	68%	$ 1,200,000	63%
		ABC	$ 750,000	$ 1,000,000	75%	$ 1,100,000	68%	$ 1,200,000	63%
	Planned Giving		$ 1,500,000	$ 2,000,000	75%	$ 2,200,000	68%	$ 2,400,000	63%
		ABC	$ 750,000	$ 1,000,000	75%	$ 1,100,000	68%	$ 1,200,000	63%
		ABC	$ 750,000	$ 1,000,000	75%	$ 1,100,000	68%	$ 1,200,000	63%
Headquarters			$ 6,000,000	$8,000,000	75%	$8,800,000	68%	$9,600,000	63%
	Corporate Partnerhips		$ 1,500,000	$ 2,000,000	75%	$ 2,200,000	68%	$ 2,400,000	63%
		ABC	$ 750,000	$ 1,000,000	75%	$ 1,100,000	68%	$ 1,200,000	63%
		ABC	$ 750,000	$ 1,000,000	75%	$ 1,100,000	68%	$ 1,200,000	63%
	Foundation Relations		$ 1,500,000	$ 2,000,000	75%	$ 2,200,000	68%	$ 2,400,000	63%
		ABC	$ 750,000	$ 1,000,000	75%	$ 1,100,000	68%	$ 1,200,000	63%
		ABC	$ 750,000	$ 1,000,000	75%	$ 1,100,000	68%	$ 1,200,000	63%
	Major Gifts		$ 1,500,000	$ 2,000,000	75%	$ 2,200,000	68%	$ 2,400,000	63%
		ABC	$ 750,000	$ 1,000,000	75%	$ 1,100,000	68%	$ 1,200,000	63%
		ABC	$ 750,000	$ 1,000,000	75%	$ 1,100,000	68%	$ 1,200,000	63%
	Planned Giving		$ 1,500,000	$ 2,000,000	75%	$ 2,200,000	68%	$ 2,400,000	63%
		ABC	$ 750,000	$ 1,000,000	75%	$ 1,100,000	68%	$ 1,200,000	63%
		ABC	$ 750,000	$ 1,000,000	75%	$ 1,100,000	68%	$ 1,200,000	63%
Maryland			$ 6,000,000	$8,000,000	75%	$8,800,000	68%	$9,600,000	63%
	Corporate Partnerhips		$ 1,500,000	$ 2,000,000	75%	$ 2,200,000	68%	$ 2,400,000	63%
		ABC	$ 750,000	$ 1,000,000	75%	$ 1,100,000	68%	$ 1,200,000	63%
		ABC	$ 750,000	$ 1,000,000	75%	$ 1,100,000	68%	$ 1,200,000	63%
	Foundation Relations		$ 1,500,000	$ 2,000,000	75%	$ 2,200,000	68%	$ 2,400,000	63%
		ABC	$ 750,000	$ 1,000,000	75%	$ 1,100,000	68%	$ 1,200,000	63%
		ABC	$ 750,000	$ 1,000,000	75%	$ 1,100,000	68%	$ 1,200,000	63%
	Major Gifts		$ 1,500,000	$ 2,000,000	75%	$ 2,200,000	68%	$ 2,400,000	63%
		ABC	$ 750,000	$ 1,000,000	75%	$ 1,100,000	68%	$ 1,200,000	63%
		ABC	$ 750,000	$ 1,000,000	75%	$ 1,100,000	68%	$ 1,200,000	63%
	Planned Giving		$ 1,500,000	$ 2,000,000	75%	$ 2,200,000	68%	$ 2,400,000	63%
		ABC	$ 750,000	$ 1,000,000	75%	$ 1,100,000	68%	$ 1,200,000	63%
		ABC	$ 750,000	$ 1,000,000	75%	$ 1,100,000	68%	$ 1,200,000	63%

Revenue Forecast Report Mock-Up

Office	Department	Staff	Donor	Stage	Revenue to Date (1)	Probaility (2)	Forecast (3)	Total Estimated Annual Revenue	Good Annual Fundraising Goal	Percentage of Good Goal Achieved	Better Annual Fundraising Goal	Percentage of Better Goal Achieved	Best Annual Fundraising Goal	Percentage of Best Goal Achieved
Organization					$		$		$	%	$	%	$	%
California					$		$	$	$	%	$	%	$	%
	Corporate Partnerhips				$		$	$	$	%	$	%	$	%
		ABC			$		$	$	$	%	$	%	$	%
			ABC		$	%	$	$	$	%	$	%	$	%
			ABC		$	%	$	$	$	%	$	%	$	%
			ABC		$	%	$	$	$	%	$	%	$	%
		ABC			$		$	$	$	%	$	%	$	%
			ABC		$	%	$	$	$	%	$	%	$	%
			ABC		$	%	$	$	$	%	$	%	$	%
			ABC		$	%	$	$	$	%	$	%	$	%
	Foundation Relations				$		$	$	$	%	$	%	$	%
		ABC			$		$	$	$	%	$	%	$	%
		ABC			$		$	$	$	%	$	%	$	%
	Major Gifts				$		$	$	$	%	$	%	$	%
		ABC			$		$	$	$	%	$	%	$	%
		ABC			$		$	$	$	%	$	%	$	%
	Planned Giving				$		$	$	$	%	$	%	$	%
		ABC			$		$	$	$	%	$	%	$	%
		ABC			$		$	$	$	%	$	%	$	%
Headquarters					$		$	$	$	%	$	%	$	%
	Corporate Partnerhips				$		$	$	$	%	$	%	$	%
		ABC			$		$	$	$	%	$	%	$	%
		ABC			$		$	$	$	%	$	%	$	%
	Foundation Relations				$		$	$	$	%	$	%	$	%
		ABC			$		$	$	$	%	$	%	$	%
		ABC			$		$	$	$	%	$	%	$	%
	Major Gifts				$		$	$	$	%	$	%	$	%
		ABC			$		$	$	$	%	$	%	$	%
		ABC			$		$	$	$	%	$	%	$	%
	Planned Giving				$		$	$	$	%	$	%	$	%
		ABC			$		$	$	$	%	$	%	$	%
		ABC			$		$	$	$	%	$	%	$	%
Maryland					$		$	$	$	%	$	%	$	%
	Corporate Partnerhips				$		$	$	$	%	$	%	$	%
		ABC			$		$	$	$	%	$	%	$	%
		ABC			$		$	$	$	%	$	%	$	%
	Foundation Relations				$		$	$	$	%	$	%	$	%
		ABC			$		$	$	$	%	$	%	$	%
		ABC			$		$	$	$	%	$	%	$	%
	Major Gifts				$		$	$	$	%	$	%	$	%
		ABC			$		$	$	$	%	$	%	$	%
		ABC			$		$	$	$	%	$	%	$	%
	Planned Giving				$		$	$	$	%	$	%	$	%
		ABC			$		$	$	$	%	$	%	$	%
		ABC			$		$	$	$	%	$	%	$	%

(1) Includes Strategic Relationship Management Cycles in the Gift Processing, Acknowledgement & Recognition and Stewardship stages.
(2) Probabiilty in many CRM systems is calculated based on a % likelihood of securing the gift associated with the stage of the Strategic Relationship Management Cycle. In an ideal world this would be a configurable algorithm that takes into account the prospect's Capacity, Interst, Alignment, and Connection ratings and the Ask Readiness Rating associated with the Strategic Relationship Management Cycle.
(3) Includes Strategic Relationship Management Cycles in the Strategy, Cultivation, and Solicitation stages.

Strategic Interaction Tracking Report Mock-Up

Prospect Name
Strategic Relationship Management Cycle

Type of Interaction*	Date	Assigned To	Status	Highlights of the Interaction
Last Three Completed Strategic Interactions				
ABC	MM/DD/YY	ABC	ABC	ABC
ABC	MM/DD/YY	ABC	ABC	ABC
ABC	MM/DD/YY	ABC	ABC	ABC
Next Three Scheduled Strategic Interactions				
ABC	MM/DD/YY	ABC	ABC	ABC
ABC	MM/DD/YY	ABC	ABC	ABC
ABC	MM/DD/YY	ABC	ABC	ABC

**Your organization should determine which types of interactions are strategic (e.g., phone conversation, face-to-face meeting, mission experience) and include only those on this report.*

Solicitor Credit Report Mock-Up

Relationship Manager
Role

Constituent Name	Cycle	Type of Gift*	Gift Amount	Timeframe of Gift	Date Funds Committed	Date Funds Received
ABC						
	ABC	ABC	$	# year(s)	MM/DD/YY	MM/DD/YY
	ABC	ABC	$	# year(s)	MM/DD/YY	MM/DD/YY
ABC						
	ABC	ABC	$	# year(s)	MM/DD/YY	MM/DD/YY
ABC						
	ABC	ABC	$	# year(s)	MM/DD/YY	MM/DD/YY
ABC						
		ABC	$	# year(s)	MM/DD/YY	MM/DD/YY
		ABC	$	# year(s)	MM/DD/YY	MM/DD/YY
ABC						
		ABC	$	# year(s)	MM/DD/YY	MM/DD/YY

Note: Report should be sorted in descending order by Gift Amount so transformational gifts appear at the top.

Assist Credit Report Mock-Up

Staff Person
Role

Constituent Name	Strategic Relationship Management Cycle	Total Gift Amount	Type of Interaction*	Date	Status	Highlights of the Interaction
ABC						
	ABC	$				
			ABC	MM/DD/YY	ABC	ABC
			ABC	MM/DD/YY	ABC	ABC
			ABC	MM/DD/YY	ABC	ABC
	ABC	$				
			ABC	MM/DD/YY	ABC	ABC
			ABC	MM/DD/YY	ABC	ABC
			ABC	MM/DD/YY	ABC	ABC
ABC						
	ABC	$				
			ABC	MM/DD/YY	ABC	ABC
			ABC	MM/DD/YY	ABC	ABC
			ABC	MM/DD/YY	ABC	ABC
ABC						
	ABC	$				
	ABC		ABC	MM/DD/YY	ABC	ABC
	ABC		ABC	MM/DD/YY	ABC	ABC
	ABC		ABC	MM/DD/YY	ABC	ABC

About Lisa Scott

Author Photo by Zhee Chatmon

Lisa Scott is President of TGP Consulting, a company dedicated to helping nonprofit organizations working towards a just, equitable, and sustainable world raise more money so they can do even more good. What makes TGP Consulting different is the experience and expertise we bring to help you build both the institutional and individual infrastructure required to achieve big, bold goals.

Before launching TGP Consulting, Lisa was a Co-Founder and Partner with Barker & Scott Consulting, one of the nation's leading management consulting and technology strategy firms serving nonprofit organizations.

Lisa's experience with many of the world's largest and most prestigious nonprofits over the past 20 years has given her in-depth insights into the power six and seven-figure gifts have to transform an organization's impact, along with the organization itself, the people within the organization, and the donors themselves.

In 2022, Lisa was awarded one of the nonprofit industry's inaugural 40 Over 40 Awards, which celebrates the dedicated professionals who consistently set a high bar for excellence in the nonprofit sector–elevating the organizations, the people around them, and the lives of the people who want to make a difference in the world.

In *The Transformational Giving Playbook*™ Lisa delivers a powerful framework for how nonprofits can use the science of fundraising to elevate the art and move from incremental to exponential growth in revenue and mission impact.

Endnotes

1 We did not list donor-advised funds; however, these types of donor collectives represent a growing segment of donors for some nonprofits. We recommend organizations focus on the trustees of donor-advised funds along with any "gatekeepers" who can facilitate introductions to some of the families within a donor-advised fund who are interested in your mission.

2 We first learned about the idea of a tiered goal setting process, as well as what is and isn't controllable, from Todd Herman's *90-Day Year: The Ultimate Peak*. We have taken this process and expanded and adapted it for nonprofits.

3 Planned gifts are an exception to this rule. Many nonprofits may solicit planned gifts as part of their Direct Marketing program, and this book does not address Direct Marketing fundraising; however, it might be appropriate to create a Strategic Relationship Management Cycle(s) for planned gifts where you anticipate a transformational gift from an estate. The difference between a planned gift cycle vs. other cycles is: a smaller cultivation team is typically involved, the strategic interactions carried out during cultivation might be more standard across prospects and less tailored, and the Cultivation stage could last many years.

4 Storytellers of all kinds have been using the Hook-Book-Look-Took formula with great success for decades. The concept originated in the theological world, in a 1976 book by Lawrence Richards titled, *Creative Bible Teaching* (Moody Publishing).

Printed in the USA
CPSIA information can be obtained
at www.ICGtesting.com
LVHW061538061123
762867LV00028B/143/J

9 781956 867701